VALIANT IN THE
TESTIMONY OF CHRIST

VALIANT IN THE TESTIMONY OF CHRIST

JOSEPH FIELDING MCCONKIE

Ben Haven Books

Send inquiries to:

info@McConkieBooks.com

For additional titles from this author visit www.McConkieBooks.com

Printed in the United States of America

ISBN: 978-1-934537-53-4

Interior by Jonathon R. Owen (Spanish Fork, Utah)
Cover designed by Brent R. Nordgren (Provo, Utah) and Jonathon R. Owen

CONTENTS

CONTENTS

PREFACE

This work centers in the testimony of Christ that we as Latter-day Saints have been commissioned to bear to all the peoples and nations of the earth. Our testimony is substantially different than that borne by those of other faiths. It embraces a marvelous host of truths not known to them, truths distinctive to the revelations of the Restoration. These truths bring with them light and joy and that will, as they become known, cause faith to increase throughout the earth. The work is motivated by the concern that as a people we do not recognize the strength and power of that which we have been given, while there are many who seek after these truths but simply do not know where to find them.

We cannot testify of what we do not know. It matters not how much the Lord has given us if we are not familiar with it. In 1832 the Lord told the Latter-day Saint people that their minds "in times past" had been "darkened because of unbelief" because they had "treated lightly" the revelations they had received. This "vanity and unbelief," the Lord said, placed the "whole church under condemnation." The condemnation was to remain until they repented and gained a knowledge and testimony of the things given them in the revelations of the Restoration and in the Book of Mormon (see D&C 84:54–57). Whether that condemnation still rests upon us or not I will leave to others to decide, but that we are largely unaware of the significance of the revelations we have received relative to our testimony of Christ is painfully evident. It is true that we have in recent years become more conscious of the theological significance of the Atonement and have paid more verbal homage to it. Whether this represents a deeper gospel understanding or is simply a fashionable practice we follow so that we might be in the image and likeness of the world is again a question which I will not presume to answer.

The matter upon which I have no right to remain silent, however, as a Latter-day Saint is that our testimony both individually and collectively must reflect a knowledge of the marvelous truths about Christ that are uniquely and distinctly ours. That is to say, because there was a Joseph Smith, because there is a Book of Mormon, because we have a host of revealed truths about Christ in the revelations of the Restoration unknown to the Bible-believing world, we are obligated to testify of Christ in a manner which in purity and power reaches far beyond that which can be borne by any other person or people on the face of the earth. For our testimony to be less than this is, as the Lord stated it, to "pollute [his] holy land." While the promise given us is that if we are steadfast and true in bearing testimony of these principles our sins will be forgiven and our tongues loosed that we might have the "power of God unto the convincing of men" (D&C 11:21; see also D&C 84:58–61).

Competence as a witness is predicated on knowledge. If you do not know anything, you cannot testify to anything. To testify is to teach. A testimony is an expression of light and truth. The greater your light the more powerful your testimony. This work is written to the end that we might bear a more powerful testimony of Christ, one equal to the trust placed in us long before we were born and renewed again at the time of our baptism. It is our responsibility and privilege to be both competent and confident witnesses of him whose name we have covenanted to bear.

Among some the prince of darkness has found success in denying the Christ; among others his success is in presenting false Christs. This has a double advantage: the deluded, supposing themselves to be clothed in the robes of righteousness, now march at his command, while those who see through his delusion become hardened against the idea that there might indeed be a true and living Church and thus a true and living Christ. Among the true Saints, those blessed with a knowledge of Christ rooted in true principles, there are those who have been paralyzed into inaction by the notion that it would be unchristian to speak against those who seek to destroy them. Then there are those who bring "a railing accusation" against the adversary and thus unwittingly become his disciples because they are actuated by his spirit.

What then is our responsibility? Can we just avoid the fray, lose ourselves in other things and act as if it is not really an issue? Or is it a covenant responsibility, one first made long before we were born, to stand and be counted where the testimony of Christ is concerned? Are we not all sobered by the declaration in the revelation on the degrees of glory wherein it describes those who inherit the terrestrial kingdom saying, "These are they who are not valiant in the testimony of Jesus; wherefore, they obtain not the crown over the kingdom of our God" (D&C 76:79).

To be "valiant in the testimony of Jesus" is to be bold and courageous. The word *valiant* shares the same Latin root as such words as *valid*, *validate*, *valor*, and *value*, all of which carry the meaning "to be strong." By its very nature, a testimony cannot be neutral or lack the power of conviction. It is a declaration of that for which we stand. To bear testimony is to choose sides in the battle over religious truths. If the Holy Ghost is your companion, you cannot lack for boldness. The Holy Ghost is neither hesitant nor tentative.

The greatest lessons we learn in this life are taught us by way of contrast. For instance, it is only when something is taken from us that we fully appreciate its importance to us. The temporary loss of sight, hearing, or memory brings unmeasured rejoicing at its restoration. So it is with the loss of health in any form. Sore muscles, sleepless nights, or pangs of hunger, like countless other difficulties, each bring their reminder of that which otherwise goes unappreciated. Separation from a loved one brings with it a heightened appreciation of his or her importance to us. The threat of losing any good thing brings with it a greater appreciation of its importance.

Jacob tells us that if no Atonement had been made, we would all be devils, or angels to a devil, having no power to free ourselves from the enslavement of death and sin. This understanding gives us a greater appreciation for the atoning sacrifice of Christ than we could otherwise have (see 2 Nephi 9:9). Alma describes the manner in which his soul was "racked with eternal torment," as he suffered the "pains of hell." His soul, he said was racked with "inexpressible horror" even to the extent that he desired to be "extinct both soul and body." He then tells us of the joy he found in his acceptance of Christ. "My soul was filled with joy as exceeding as was my pain!" he said. Thus with great effect he teaches us that there is no sin worth committing and also of the power that is in Christ to lift the burden of sin from us (see Alma 36:12–21).

None taught by contrast with greater effect than Christ himself. In the Sermon on the Mount, for instance, he repetitiously said something to the effect of "it hath been said by them of old thus and thus, but I say unto this and this," and thus he contrasted the old covenant with the new. The doctrines of the Book of Mormon are taught in the conflict between the Nephites and Lamanites; the Old Testament story contrasts the power of Israel's God with the gods of the neighboring nations; the New Testament places Christ in conflict with the Great Sanhedrin and a corrupted temple priesthood.

From the Book of Moses we learn how Israel's great prophet was transfigured so that he might stand in God's presence and then how that glory was withdrawn, leaving Moses to say, "Now, for this cause I know that man is nothing." Satan is then allowed to seek Moses' discipleship causing Moses to ask, "Where is thy glory, that I should worship thee? For behold, I could not look upon God, except his glory should come upon me, and I were transfigured before him. But I can look upon thee in the natural man. Is it not so, surely?" (Moses 1:13–14) The lesson was well taught for we now hear Moses declaring now, "I can judge between thee and God" (Moses 1:15). Such is the pattern we find in the First Vision as the youthful Joseph Smith is engulfed in darkness before he is delivered by a glorious light from heaven. Again we see the pattern in the revelation on the degrees of glory where a description of those who become perdition is contrasted with the celestial kingdom, and the celestial kingdom is contrasted in turn with the terrestrial and telestial worlds.

Near countless illustrations can be given, but we will let it suffice to say that no gospel principle can be fully understood or appreciated save we have seen its opposite or have some understanding of what it would be like to be without it.

As a people we cannot see and understand the greatness and glory of that which the Lord has restored to us through the Prophet Joseph Smith and the revelations of the Restoration save we see them at least in some measure contrasted with the state of man at the time they were restored. Again, you do not realize what you have until you have some idea of what it would be like to be without it. Thus it is that those brought into the faith can be more appreciative of it than those born and raised amid the splendor of gospel light. The experience of a mission can deepen our appreciation of the gospel when we see what life for others is like without the gospel.

The strength and power of the doctrines of which this work speaks, doctrines fundamental to our testimony of Christ, cannot be taught without making some contrast with the false doctrines of historical Christianity. No disrespect to the good people of other faiths is intended by stating the doctrines espoused by their churches. Consider that many nations have systems of government that deny basic human rights to their citizens. All such systems are corrupt, and their practices an abomination in the sight of God. In so saying, I am not condemning the people of those nations, but I am declaring my concern for them as God's children and as my brothers and sisters. As it is with nations, so it is with churches. If I have food and they are starving, I have an obligation by the very fact that I breathe to share what I have with them, and if I have truth that exceeds their own of the plan of salvation, then my obligation can be none the less. As to truth, we must clearly see it if we are to clearly teach it; we must, like Moses and Joseph Smith, be shown both the darkness and the light that we might never confuse the two.

ACKNOWLEDGMENTS

Impressed with both the need for a work such as this and with my own inadequacy to do it, I turned to a trusted friend, Robert J. Matthews, for support. His careful review of the doctrines taught is a source of considerable assurance. I'm grateful to Jay A. Parry, who has served as editor. I am also much in debt to Richard Neitzel Holzapfel, publications director of the Religious Studies Center at Brigham Young University, and to his competent staff, including Camber N. Agrelius, Jacob F. Frandsen, Amanda K. Fronk, R. Devan Jensen, James D. Jensen, Brent R. Nordgren, Jonathon R. Owen, Joany O. Pinegar, Rosie E. Ricks, and Dayna K. Thomas.

I express my deepest appreciation to my brother Mark, who offered many helpful suggestions. Thanks goes to my son Nathan for all his energetic help and to Boyd Tuttle of Digital Legend for his services as publisher. Matthew B. Christensen is also to be thanked for more reasons than I can remember.

CHAPTER 1

YOUR TESTIMONY

THERE is nothing in this entire world that equals in value the testimony you have of the gospel of Jesus Christ. Your testimony is the composite of all you know and all you have experienced in the realm of spiritual things. It is your testimony that makes you what you are, and it is your testimony that will rise with you in the resurrection. As you walk by the light of your testimony in this life, so will you walk by that same light in the worlds to come. Alma stated the matter well: "That same spirit which doth possess your bodies at the time that ye go out of this life, that same spirit will have power to possess your body in that eternal world" (Alma 34:34). The spirit that possesses your body is the light that comes from the testimony of the gospel that is yours. You walk by that light, you pray by that light, you teach by that light, and you make every choice of consequence in your life by that same light.

DEFINING TESTIMONY

Your testimony is a living thing, and, as such, it requires the nourishment and care necessary to the sustaining of life. The source of that life is the spirit of revelation. If you were to lose this spirit, your testimony would shrivel and die; conversely, as that same spirit is found in your life, it will continue to grow "brighter and brighter until the perfect day" (D&C 50:24). John the Revelator declared that "the testimony of Jesus is the spirit of prophecy" (Revelation 19:10). Without the "spirit of prophecy" you cannot have a testimony. All who enjoy that spirit are, in their own right, prophets or prophetesses.

As Joseph Smith explained,

> If any person should ask me if I were a prophet, I should not deny it, as that would give me the lie; for, according to John, the testimony of Jesus is the spirit of prophecy; therefore, if I profess to be a witness or teacher, and have not the spirit of prophecy, which is the testimony of Jesus, I must be a false witness; but if I be a true teacher and witness, I must possess the spirit of prophecy, and that constitutes a prophet; and any man who says he is a teacher or preacher of righteousness, and denies the spirit of prophecy, is a liar, and the truth is not in him; and by this key false teachers and impostors may be detected.[1]

To have the power of salvation in it, our testimony must be borne of the Spirit, and it must conform to the laws and ordinances of the gospel, for without these ordinances a saving testimony cannot be had. Of necessity the Lord's people have always been a covenant people. For instance, Nephi, in describing the gathering of Israel in the last days, said, "At that day shall the remnant of our seed know that they are of the house of Israel, and that they are the covenant people of the Lord; and then shall they know and come to the knowledge of their forefathers, and also to the knowledge of the gospel of their Redeemer . . . ; wherefore, they shall come to the knowledge of their Redeemer and the very points of his doctrine, that they may know how to come unto him and be saved" (1 Nephi 15:14).

Nephi is telling us that it is only in the covenant that a testimony of Christ (such a testimony as has the power of salvation in it) can be obtained. For instance, you must enter into the covenant of baptism before you receive the gift of the Holy Ghost, without which gift you can neither receive nor understand the revelations of heaven. Scripture refers to the ordinances of the gospel as mysteries. The reason is twofold: first, a mystery is something that can be known only by revelation; second, the ordinances are designed as a form of revelation through which we obtain knowledge and understanding that we could not otherwise experience. This is the reason why we speak of the temple ordinance as an endowment. In the receipt of this ordinance we are endowed (clothed) with knowledge and power that we could not otherwise receive. The Spirit leads to the covenant and the covenant leads to a greater outpouring of the Spirit. Then, as we are constant in the keeping of the covenant, the Lord is constant in granting us additional light and truth.

The principle here involved finds expression in the description of those who obtain the celestial kingdom. "They are they who received the testimony of Jesus, and believed on his name and were baptized after the manner of his burial, being buried in the water in his name, and this according to the commandment which he has given—that by keeping the commandments they might be washed and cleansed from all their sins, and receive the Holy Spirit by the laying on of the hands of him who is ordained and sealed unto this power" (D&C 76:51–52). The inseparable nature of the covenants we make and the testimony we bear is again illustrated in the dedicatory prayer of the Kirtland Temple. That the testimony of the missionaries might be one of power, the Prophet importuned the Lord to "put upon thy servants the testimony of the covenant, that when they go out and proclaim thy word they may seal up the law, and prepare the hearts of [the] saints" for all that is to come (D&C 109:38).

A Testimony Requires Courage

It also ought to be observed that courage is an essential ingredient to the testimony that has the power of salvation in it. It will be recalled that the revelation on the degrees of glory tells us that numbered among those in the terrestrial kingdom will be those who were "not valiant in the testimony of Jesus; wherefore, they obtain not the crown over the kingdom of our God" (D&C 76:79). Courage in the bearing of testimony is also identified as the criterion or reservoir into which the knowledge of heaven is dispensed among those living during the millennial era. Our scripture states that all manner of knowledge is to be "revealed and set forth upon all who have endured valiantly for the gospel of Jesus Christ" (D&C 121:29). In the vision of the redemption of the dead, we are told that the faithful who were invited to greet Christ when he came to that world were those "who had offered sacrifice in the similitude of the great sacrifice of the Son of God [that is, those who complied with the ordinance], and had suffered tribulation in their Redeemer's name. All these had departed the mortal life, firm in the hope of a glorious resurrection, through the grace of God the Father and his Only Begotten Son, Jesus Christ" (D&C 138:13–14).

If we do not have the courage of our message, the Holy Ghost will quickly leave us. President J. Reuben Clark Jr. addressed this issue in his classic discourse "The Charted Course of the Church in Education." He told us that there were "two prime things which may not be overlooked, forgotten, shaded, or discarded":

> First—that Jesus Christ is the Son of God, the Only Begotten of the Father in the flesh, the Creator of the world, the Lamb of God, the Sacrifice for the sins of the world, the Atoner for Adam's transgression; that He was crucified; that His spirit left His body; that He died; that He was laid away in the tomb; that on the third day His spirit was reunited with His body, which again became a living being; that He was raised from the tomb a resurrected being, a perfect Being, the First Fruits of the Resurrection; that He later ascended to the Father; and that because of His death and by and through His resurrection every man born into the world since the beginning will be likewise literally resurrected. This doctrine is as old as the world. Job declared: "And though after my skin worms destroy this body, yet in my flesh shall I see God: whom I shall see for myself and mine eyes shall behold, and not another." (Job 19:26–27.)
>
> The resurrected body is a body of flesh and bones and spirit, and Job was uttering a great and everlasting truth. These positive facts, and all other facts necessarily implied therein, must all be honestly believed, in full faith, by every member of the Church.
>
> The second of the two things to which we must all give full faith is that the Father and the Son actually and in truth and very deed appeared to the Prophet Joseph in a vision in the woods; that other heavenly visions followed to Joseph and to others; that the gospel and the

Holy Priesthood after the Order of the Son of God were in truth and fact restored to the earth from which they were lost by the apostasy of the primitive Church; that the Lord again set up His Church, through the agency of Joseph Smith; that the Book of Mormon is just what it professes to be; that to the Prophet came numerous revelations for guidance, upbuilding, organization, and encouragement of the Church and its members; that the Prophet's successors, likewise called of God, have received revelations as the needs of the Church have required, and that they will continue to receive revelations as the Church and its members, living the truth they already have, shall stand in need of more; that this is in truth The Church of Jesus Christ of Latter-day Saints; and that its foundation beliefs are the laws and principles laid down in the Articles of Faith. These facts also, and each of them, together with all things necessarily implied therein or flowing therefrom, must stand, unchanged, unmodified, without dilution, excuse, apology, or avoidance; they may not be explained away or submerged. Without these two great beliefs the Church would cease to be the Church.

President Clark then explained that it is not enough to have a testimony. You must also have what he referred to as "one of the rarest and most precious" of all character traits—"moral courage." Borne without courage, your testimony will be so diluted before it settles on those for whom it is intended that it will probably do more harm than good, he held. To "moral courage" President Clark said must be added "intellectual courage." This he defined as the courage to stand unmoved when the principles you are teaching do not accord well with scientific and other intellectual principles currently in vogue among the intellectual chiefs of our race. "Not unknown are cases where men of presumed faith, holding responsible positions, have felt that, since by affirming their full faith they might call down upon themselves the ridicule of their unbelieving colleagues, they must either modify or explain away their faith, or destructively dilute it, or even pretend to cast it away. Such are hypocrites to their colleagues and to their co-religionists." Speaking with a candor and directness little known to our day, President Clark said,

> For any Latter-day Saint psychologist, chemist, physicist, geologist, archeologist, or any other scientist, to explain away, or misinterpret, or evade or elude, or most of all, to repudiate or to deny, the great fundamental doctrines of the Church in which he professes to believe, is to give the lie to his intellect, to lose his self-respect, to bring sorrow to his friends, to break the hearts and bring shame to his parents, to besmirch the Church and its members, and to forfeit the respect and honor of those whom he has sought, by his course, to win as friends and helpers.[2]

SEALING A TESTIMONY

Consider the language of Joseph Smith relative to bearing testimony of Christ. Of the great revelation on the degrees of glory, which he and Sidney Rigdon saw together, he wrote:

> By the power of the Spirit our eyes were opened and our understandings were enlightened, so as to see and understand the things of God—even those things which were from the beginning before the world was, which

were ordained of the Father, through his Only Begotten Son, who was in the bosom of the Father, even from the beginning; of whom we bear record; *and the record which we bear is the fulness of the gospel of Jesus Christ,* who is the Son, whom we saw and with whom we conversed in the heavenly vision. (D&C 76:12–14; emphasis added)

Here the Prophet is telling us that his testimony of Christ is not confined to one revelatory experience or a particular principle or concept but that it embraces "the fulness of the gospel of Jesus Christ." The testimony of Joseph Smith relative to Christ encompassed all that he revealed about Christ and the principles of his gospel. We are in the habit of thinking that a testimony is the relatively brief expression of faith made in those instances in which that which we are saying has been formally introduced as our testimony. In fact, our testimony is the composite of all that we teach about Christ, not just the expression that concludes or crowns what we have taught.

At the conclusion of a semester-long class on the life of Christ, a student asked me, "Aren't you going to bear your testimony?" My response was that my testimony consisted of all that I had taught from the first day of class to the last. It cannot and should not be thought of as but a brief expression at the end of the last day of class when the teacher says, "I testify that these things are true." Everything I taught I taught because it is part of my testimony; it is what I know about Christ and his life and his ministry, his doctrine and the example he set for us. The expression "I know that what I have been teaching is true" is a seal that I place on what I have taught. My testimony is the composite of all that has been taught, just as the testimony we bear is the composite of all that we know and all that we are.

WHAT, THEN, IS YOUR TESTIMONY?

What, then, is your testimony? It is the knowledge you have, by the witness of the Spirit, of the principles detailed by President J. Reuben Clark in the preceding quotation. Indeed, your testimony reaches far beyond the kind of witnessing for Christ that is common in the Christian world. It centers in what you are and what you do and what you know. As a Latter-day Saint, you have the privilege of knowing a host of truths long lost to traditional Christianity relative to the divinity and mission of our Lord and Savior Jesus the Christ. Considering all that has been given us as Latter-day Saints, let us ask this question: If you were called upon to identify the most significant truths relative to Christ that we treasure as part of the Restoration, truths not had by the world, are you prepared to do it? Are you prepared to teach the rising generation and those not of our faith these sacred truths with clarity and power? Just what is your testimony of Christ? In the chapters that follow, let us consider some of the basic and fundamental truths that are essential to the testimony we bear and that give power and force to it.

NOTES

1. Smith, *Teachings*, 269.
2. Clark, "The Charted Course of the Church."

CHAPTER 2
A SON OF THE MORNING IS FALLEN

O UR testimony of Christ is limited to the knowledge and understanding we have of him and his gospel. We cannot testify to that which we do not know. Let us then set out on a venture to see what it is that we as Latter-day Saints are expected to know and understand about the saving ministry of Christ, which, had there been no restoration of the gospel, would remain unknown. Let us identify those singular truths distinctive to the restored gospel that we have been commissioned to take to those of every nation, kindred, tongue, and people; we can thereby assure that we are true to the charge given us. And let us assure that we have rejoiced in them and that we have taught them to our children. "For what doth it profit a man if a gift is bestowed upon him, and he receive not the gift? Behold, he rejoices not in that which is given unto him, neither rejoices in him who is the giver of the gift" (D&C 88:33).

Let us begin our venture in the councils of heaven, long before the foundations of this earth were laid. Here it was that we were first called upon to testify of Christ, here it was that we were first taught those principles that constitute what we know today as the gospel of Jesus Christ, and here it was that we covenanted to embrace and be true to those principles, whatever the cost, in this our second estate.

The War in Heaven

Within the pages of the Bible we find traces of two distinctive stories in which the characters involved were banished or fell from the divine presence. The first took place before the creation of the earth, the second, while it still enjoyed its paradisiacal glory. In the first instance, Isaiah likens the story of the fall of Lucifer from his heavenly glory to the fall of the king of Babylon. The way the story is told (and all other references to it) assumes that the reader is familiar with the original story, which clearly suggests that it was once a part of scripture, though our modern Bible contains but fragments of it. We turn first to the writings of Isaiah:

> How art thou fallen from heaven, O Lucifer, son of the morning! how art thou cut down to the ground, which didst weaken the nations!
>
> For thou hast said in thine heart, I will ascend into heaven, I will exalt my throne above the stars of God: I will sit also upon the mount of the congregation, in the sides of the north [on the mount of assembly, where the gods met]. (Isaiah 14:12–13)

While the text is an enigma even to Bible commentators, it seems clear that Lucifer, who we learn from other sources became Satan, was once numbered among the host of heaven, from which place he was banished for rebellion against God. While there are no other references to this event in the Old Testament, the New Testament contains an intriguing smattering of them. Christ spoke of Satan's falling from heaven (Luke 10:18) and his being "cast out" (John 12:31). Peter wrote that "God spared not the angels that sinned, but cast them down to hell, and delivered them into chains of darkness, to be reserved unto judgment" (2 Peter 2:4). Jude 1:6 expresses a similar sentiment, noting that the angels who "kept not their first estate" were destined to a place in everlasting darkness.

Revelation 12:4–12 (JST), the clearest of these texts, narrates a war in heaven which the dragon and his angels fought against the archangel Michael and his forces. The dragon, with a "third part" of the host of heaven, was banished to the earth where the war now continues. Of particular interest is that those who fought under the leadership of Michael obtained victory over the dragon "by the blood of the Lamb, and by the word of their testimony" (Revelation 12:11). Of this text one commentary notes, "The 'truth embodied in a tale' is that *the conflict between good and evil did not originate on earth but in heaven*—a very ancient belief."[1]

RESTORING THE ANCIENT BELIEF

Given that the traditional Christian world has long lost the doctrine of a premortal life and that they have no conception of a God who fathered our spirits in what we know as our "first estate," it is not to be expected that this story would be clear to them. It is clear to us as Latter-day Saints only because important parts of it have been restored to us, parts they do not have. Let us review them, doing so in the same order in which they were revealed to the Prophet Joseph Smith.

While translating the Book of Mormon, Joseph Smith dictated these words of Lehi to his scribe, Oliver Cowdery:

And I, Lehi, according to the things which I have read, must needs suppose that an angel of God, according to that which is written, had fallen from heaven; wherefore, he became a devil, having sought that which was evil before God.

And because he had fallen from heaven, and had become miserable forever, he sought also the misery of all mankind. Wherefore, he said unto Eve, yea, even that old serpent, who is the devil, who is the father of all lies, wherefore he said: Partake of the forbidden fruit, and ye shall not die, but ye shall be as God, knowing good and evil. (2 Nephi 2:17–18)

The suggestion in this text is that the principles here involved were not being taught in Lehi's day and that he discovered them in his own scriptural study.

In June 1830, as part of the restoration of the book of Genesis, these verses were revealed to Joseph Smith:

And I, the Lord God, spake unto Moses, saying: That Satan, whom thou hast commanded in the name of mine Only Begotten, is the same which was from the beginning, and he came before me, saying—Behold, here am I, send me, I will be thy son, and I will redeem all mankind, that one soul shall not be lost, and surely I will do it; wherefore give me thine honor.

But, behold, my Beloved Son, which was my Beloved and Chosen from the beginning, said unto me—Father, thy will be done, and the glory be thine forever.

Wherefore, because that Satan rebelled against me, and sought to destroy the agency of man, which I, the

Lord God, had given him, and also, that I should give unto him mine own power; by the power of mine Only Begotten, I caused that he should be cast down;

And he became Satan, yea, even the devil, the father of all lies, to deceive and to blind men, and to lead them captive at his will, even as many as would not hearken unto my voice. (Moses 4:1–4)

While the whole story is yet to be unfolded, what is of particular interest at this point is that the rebellion in heaven centered over the issue of who it was that would be chosen to redeem mankind in the capacity of God's Son. After Satan's appeal to be chosen as our Redeemer was rejected, he instigated a great heavenly revolt. In September 1830, what might be considered an addendum to this revelation was received. In the context of the story of the second fall, or that of Adam in Eden, the Lord said, "Behold, I gave unto him [Adam] that he should be an agent unto himself" (D&C 29:35). This establishes that agency, which is the power to act independently, was essential to both stories, as it is to the entire plan of salvation. Affirming this, the text says, "And it came to pass that Adam, being tempted of the devil—for, behold, the devil was before Adam, for he rebelled against me, saying, Give me thine honor, which is my power; and also a third part of the hosts of heaven turned he away from me because of their agency; and they were thrust down, and thus came the devil and his angels; and, behold, there is a place prepared for them from the beginning, which place is hell" (D&C 29:36–38).

In February 1832 the revelation we have come to know as "the Vision" expanded our story even further. In this revelation Joseph Smith and Sidney Rigdon were shown "an angel of God who was in authority in the presence of God, who rebelled against the Only Begotten Son . . . [and] was thrust down from the presence of God and the Son and was called Perdition, for the heavens wept over him—he was Lucifer, a son of the morning" (D&C 76:25–26). That is, he was once a bright and shining star, but he fell from his high place. The name Lucifer means "light," or "torch bearer," while the appellation "son of the morning" suggests either that he was one of the early born or that he was one of the bright and shining stars or perhaps both. In any event, he was obviously one of the great and revered spirits.

Still, more revelation would be necessary before the story could be brought into sharp focus. A revelation received in 1833 announced that "man was also in the beginning with God" (D&C 93:29). This had to wait until the publication of the book of Abraham, which took place in Nauvoo in 1842. It is Abraham's record that makes it clear that all humankind were born first as the spirit children of God in a premortal estate, in which they prepared themselves for the experiences that would be theirs in mortality. The key verses of this revelation take on meaning in the light of the verses that had been restored before them.

"And the Lord said: Whom shall I send? And one answered like unto the Son of Man: Here am I, send me. And another answered and said: Here am I, send me. And the Lord said: I will send the first. And the second was angry, and kept not his first estate; and, at that day, many followed after him" (Abraham 3:27–28).

If it had not been for the other revelations that we had been given, these verses would have been as puzzling to us as the Isaiah text with which we began is to the sectarian world.

From Abraham we learn that the noble and great spirits assisted Christ in the creation of the earth. Combining the Abraham text and the other texts that have been restored, we learn that following the creation of the earth, a grand council was held in heaven, at which the Father explained why the earth had been created. Thus he reviewed with all his spirit children the plan of salvation, including the necessity of their coming to earth to be tried and tested to see if they would do all things that they were commanded. All, they were told, who kept their first estate, meaning would not join the army of rebellion and be cast out with Lucifer, would be "added upon"; that is, they would obtain physical bodies like unto those of their divine parents and become rightful heirs of all the power and glory that their parents possessed. Thus they were assured that by keeping their second estate, they would "have glory added upon their heads for ever and ever" (Abraham 3:26).

TELL THE STORY WELL

This story, which is well known to Latter-day Saints, frequently gets told incorrectly. Often it has been said that two plans were presented for the Father's consideration, one by Christ and one by Lucifer. It is important to note that the Father did not make an appeal for plans or suggestions as to how man ought to be saved. The question he asked was not, "What shall I do?" but rather, "Whom shall I send?" Christ was chosen because he desired to willingly do the will of the Father in all things. His response as recorded by Moses was, "Father, thy will be done, and the glory be thine forever" (Moses 4:2). From the very beginning, the whole concept of salvation as known to Latter-day Saints centers in obedience to the will of the Father, Christ being the perfect example of this principle.

The antithesis of this is the idea that either he or they could be saved by anything less than their rendering complete obedience to their divine Father. Satan rebelled because Christ, the firstborn of the Father, was chosen to be our Redeemer. He sought his older brother's birthright and rebelled when it was not given to him. True it is that he proposed an unconditional salvation, but that proposal was not placed before us to decide. It could not have been. Without free will or agency as here described, there could be no plan of salvation.

"Why," it may be asked, "did the Father bother to ask whom he should send? The account itself tells us that Christ had been chosen from the beginning." Would not the answer be that as all else in heaven must be a free-will offering, so it must be with the greatest of all offerings?

It is also often mistakenly said that Satan intended to force us to be righteous. No such utterance fell from his lips, nor did he possess any such desire. There is no such thing as "forced" righteousness. "I will redeem all mankind," Satan said, "that one soul shall not be lost." Universal salvation, or salvation without works, is what was being suggested here. When agency has been surrendered, there are no choices to be made, and there can be no such thing as good or evil, only submission.

As to Our Testimony

Thus our testimony of Christ, the witness we bear of him, is distinctly different from that being borne in the traditional Christian world. The Christ of whom we speak is a spirit son of God in the same sense that we are God's spirit children. Christ is our elder brother and the firstborn of our Father in the premortal estate. He was chosen to be God's Only Begotten Son in the flesh because, of all the spirit hosts of heaven, he was the most willing to do the will of the Father. We know, then, of at least three reasons why Christ would have been chosen as our Redeemer and Savior. First, he was the firstborn and thus, if worthy, had that right by birth; second, he had a perfect understanding of the will of the Father; and third, in all things he desired to follow the will of the Father.

Given that the idea is so deeply entrenched in the minds of Latter-day Saints that God's love is the same for all his children, I hardly dare point out the obvious truth the scriptures repeatedly state. Christ is constantly spoken of by the Father as his "Beloved Son." No one seems confused as to who is being referred to when this expression is used. But a better understanding of this expression will bring with it a better understanding of the Father's choice of Christ to be our Redeemer. Describing events in the Grand Council, where the Father chose the Son, the Father said, "My Beloved Son, which was my Beloved and Chosen from the beginning, said unto me—Father, thy will be done, and the glory be thine forever" (Moses 4:2). Clearly there was no question in the Father's mind as to whom he was going to choose, even before the question was asked. Thus, the question was not asked to resolve the issue in the Father's mind. It was asked so that Christ could exercise his agency in responding. All who were in harmony with the Spirit would have known the answer to the question even before any words were spoken. The description of this event was given by Joseph Smith and Sidney Rigdon: "And this we saw also, and bear record, that an angel of God who was in authority in the presence of God, who rebelled against the Only Begotten Son whom the Father loved and who was in the bosom of the Father, was thrust down from the presence of God and the Son" (D&C 76:25).

Note how these two great spirits are described. Lucifer is a bright and shining star who is in a position of authority. By contrast, no reference is made to Christ holding such a position. He is simply spoke of as being "in the bosom of the Father" and being loved of the Father. To be at one with God and to be loved of the Father are not equated with a position of stature or with "being in authority." There is a love that the Father had for the premortal Christ, who was to be chosen as his "Only Begotten," which exceeds all other parental love. Whenever the Father introduced Christ from the heavens, he did so by saying, "This is my Beloved Son" (Matthew 3:17; 3 Nephi 11:7; D&C 93:16; JS–H 1:17).

Now, we do not have people asking, "Who could this possibly mean? We know that he loves us all the same." The answer is clear. Mormon ties the matter down by referring to Christ as the Father's "most loved Son" (Mormon 5:13). This distinction affirms our place as spirit sons and daughters of God, but it also brings with it the suggestion that Christ was the *most* loved because he was the most obedient and the most righteous of all the spirit children of God. His life in premortality and his life on earth centered on works of righteousness. These principles have been lost to those in the sectarian world and are known to us only by latter-day revelation.

In the heavenly rebellion, it was Michael the archangel who led the armies of the Lord. By revelation the Prophet Joseph Smith told us that Michael was our father, Adam (D&C 27:11). He further told us that Father Adam led the armies of the Lord in the battle in heaven, in which those who rebelled against the Father's choice of Christ to be God's Only Begotten Son were cast out (D&C 29:26; 88:112; 107:54). Further, since Adam was called the archangel, which means chief angel, we understand that Adam ranked in the heavenly army as its commanding officer. Scripture names no other archangels. Thus, Michael or Adam was the head under Christ, which position he holds to this present day. Of all the other spirit children of God, Adam thus becomes the chief witness of Christ and his greatest defender.

The example of Adam also means that our testimony of Christ was established in heaven and is but renewed here on earth. Indeed, it is our faith that all who are born into mortality have obtained the privilege to be "added upon," or to obtain bodies, because they chose to sustain Christ as our Redeemer and Savior before they were born. Those who testify of him here testified of him there. All that is embraced in a testimony of Christ was known to them and experienced by them before they were born. Such is the beginning of the testimony we bear of Christ.

NOTE

1. *Abingdon Bible Commentary*, 1386.

CHAPTER 3

A FALL TO DARKNESS

THE story of our premortal life embraces the story of the Creation and then is followed by that of Adam and Eve in Eden and their fall. Both stories are very much a part of our story. We must understand the state or status of things after they were created if we are to understand what Adam and Eve fell from, for it is the Fall that creates the need for the Atonement. Had Adam not fallen, Christ would not have risen. The purpose of the Atonement is to rectify the effects of the Fall. The Fall and the Atonement are as closely associated as the immersion in water and the emersion forth from the water are in the ordinance of baptism. The burial in water is in similitude of the death of the old man of sin, and the coming forth out of the water is in similitude of the resurrection or coming forth into a newness of life (D&C 128:12), both take place at the hands of the priesthood.

THE STORY OF EDEN

We will yet take a closer look at the Eden story and that which it represents. At this point, it will suffice for us to identify what the Bible tells us and what it does not. The book of Genesis begins with the story of earth's creation, the high point of which is the creation of the man Adam and the woman Eve. It is profoundly important to all that follows in the holy book that we understand that the first man and the first woman were created in the image and likeness of God and that they were given dominion over all other created things (Genesis 1:26–28). Had they not been in God's image, endowed with divine intelligence, they could not have been the agents of the Fall. Neither animal nor the evolutionary offspring of an animal could have brought about the Fall. The doctrine of the Fall refutes creative evolution in any form. To fall is to go from a higher state to a lower state. To evolve is to do the opposite.

After the earth was created, Adam was placed in the Garden of Eden with the command to dress and keep it. He was told that he could eat of every tree in the garden except the tree of the knowledge of good and evil, for in the day he partook of that tree he would "surely die" (Genesis 2:17). The Lord then, in conversation with someone left unidentified, observes that it is not good that the man be alone. We are told the story of Eve's creation from Adam's rib and his declaration that she was bone of his bone and flesh of his flesh. The two were married by God, who instructed Adam to leave his father and mother, a more significant phrase than it appears, and "cleave unto his wife" (Genesis 2:24) and become one flesh with her, which repeats the statement made at the time of their creation—that they were to multiply and replenish the earth.

Thereafter Eve, as Adam had named her, was persuaded by the serpent to eat of the tree of the knowledge of good and evil and prevailed upon her husband to do likewise. Now discovering that they were naked, they made themselves aprons of fig leaves and sought to hide themselves from the Lord. God called them to accountability and then cursed the serpent to crawl upon his belly and to eat the dust of the earth.

The first messianic prophecy was then uttered. Addressing the serpent, the Lord said, "I will put enmity between thee and the woman, and between thy seed and her seed" (Genesis 3:15). The meaning seems clear. Those choosing Satan as their father would have their moment of glory, and they would bruise the Savior's heel; while Eve's seed was to bruise or crush Satan's head. Obviously the ultimate victory would rest with the seed of the woman. Eve was then cursed to bear children in sorrow and pain and to be in subjection to the man; the earth was cursed for Adam's sake, in that he would have to bring forth its fruits by the sweat of his brow amid thorns and thistles. God then clothed the two of them in coats of skins and sent them out into the lone and dreary world, placing a set of angels with flaming swords in the way to prevent their returning to partake of the tree of life (see Genesis 2–3; Moses 3–4).

The story is well told, but it does nothing more than account for the loss of Eden or Paradise and explain how these two children of God became subject to death. The following chapter tells the story of Cain and Abel, after which Adam, Eve, and the Eden story are virtually lost to the interest of holy writ for some four thousand years, until Paul chose to make reference to them in three of his epistles (see Romans 5:12–14; 1 Corinthians 15:22, 45; 1 Timothy 2:13–14).

The Bible Does Not Tell Us Why Adam Fell

As we have just seen, it is from the Bible that we learn the story of the Fall. What is missing, however, is an explanation of why Adam fell and its implication as far as his descendants are concerned. The doctrine of the Fall is simply not taught in the Old Testament. This is the reason why the Jews and others whose scriptural loyalty is limited to the Old Testament have no knowledge of this doctrine. From the writings of Paul we learn that the Fall brought death and that through Christ we will again be restored to life (see 1 Corinthians 15:22). Beyond this declaration, the pages of the New Testament are also silent on this matter. You may search the Bible from now to doomsday, and you will not find within its pages such a simple thing as a definition of resurrection.

Pick up the Bible dictionary or encyclopedia of your choice and look for an entry for the Fall. The probability is that you will not find one. In fact you have a better chance of finding an article on falcons or fallow-deer. Yet without the Fall there would be no need for the Atonement. The purpose of the Atonement was to rectify the effects of the Fall; but what are they? The Bible does not tell us.

As to the Atonement, the word is found but once in the New Testament and that with the simple statement that the Saints in Rome to whom Paul was writing had been "reconciled to God" through the Atonement of Christ (see Romans 5:10–11). By contrast, the revelations of the Restoration contain more than sixty direct references to the Fall and the Atonement, with a host of attendant passages, not to mention that they also give a very plain and clear understanding of the resurrection.

AUGUSTINE AND ORIGINAL SIN

Where holy writ is silent, the philosophies of men wax eloquent. Nowhere is this more evident than on the doctrine of the Fall. Where the light of heaven has withdrawn or been hidden, darkness reigns. The doctrine of the Fall embraced by most of the Western Christian world traces back to the great Catholic theologian and philosopher Saint Augustine of Hippo (AD 354–430). Augustine authored the doctrine of "original sin," or as it is variously called, "inherited sin" or "ancestral sin." The basic idea is that of the total depravity of man, growing out of the idea that all men were part of Adam's sin in partaking of the forbidden fruit.

The scriptural text that bears the weight of Augustine's argument came from the last phrase in Romans 5:12, as rendered in the Latin Vulgate translation. Referring to the Fall of Adam, it reads, "in whom all have sinned." From this text Augustine reasoned that all of us, that is, all the children of Adam, in some way were involved in his sin and thus are equally responsible for it. We sinned with Adam. Thus "original sin" is our sin. Augustine "supposed a sort of pre-existence of all the posterity of Adam in himself so that they actually and personally sinned in him, though not, indeed, with individual consciousness . . . our sin and guilt and physical death, is a penalty even upon infant children, as it was a penalty upon Adam. The posterity of Adam therefore suffer punishment not for the sin of another but for the sin which they themselves committed in Adam."[1]

After more than a thousand years of argument and debate, the doctrine of original or inherited sin, along with the attendant idea of infant baptism, was sustained by the Council of Trent (1545–63). The Council concluded that if anyone says that Adam, "soiled by his sin of disobedience, transmitted, to all mankind only death and the pains of the body, but not sin, which is the death of the soul, let him be anathema."[2] Anathema is a formal ecclesiastical curse, accompanied by excommunication.

What is of particular interest here is that it is universally agreed that Romans 5:12 was mistranslated by Saint Jerome in the Latin Vulgate Bible. Augustine was fluent in Latin but knew little of Greek. When translators went back to the Greek from which the Latin had been translated, they discovered that the text did not carry the meaning that Augustine had appended to it. The translators of the King James Bible, instead of rendering the text "in whom all have sinned," rendered it "for [because] that all have sinned," thus the idea was shifted from all having sinned through Adam to all becoming sinners like Adam.

Modern translations, including Catholic translations, uniformly correct Jerome's error. Th e most generally accepted translation is "because" or "inasmuch" as "everyone has sinned." Wycliffe (1388), in the first English translation of the Bible, repeats the error of the Latin text from which he translated. Tyndale (1534), who gave the English-speaking world the first translation that jumped over the Catholic text and went back to the Greek, rendered the text, "insomuch that all men sinned," thus paving the way for the King James translators to make the similar change. Before this the Puritans, who came to America with their Geneva Bible (1599) and their strong Calvinistic views, had the old Latin rendering "in whom all men have sinned." Th eir footnote reads: "From Adam, in whom all have sinned, both guiltiness and death (which is the punishment of the guiltiness) came upon us all." In his *The Original New Testament: A Radical Reinterpretation and New Translation,* Hugh J. Schonfield renders the text essentially as the King James translators did. Joseph Smith in the JST leaves the King James translation unchanged.

THEOLOGICAL DARKNESS

What we have here is one of the darkest doctrines ever known, being postulated from an errant text. As truth begets truth, so error begets error. According to this doctrine, which again is fundamental to the traditions of most of the Western Christian churches, man was born in a condition of sinfulness and is thus evil by nature. Fruits of this doctrine include the damnation of all who die without being redeemed either through sacraments or personal acceptance of Christ (this, whether they had the opportunity to hear the gospel or not); the necessity of infant baptism; the subjection of women; the denigration of Adam and Eve; and the doctrine of immaculate conception.

The revelations of the Restoration help us to see these things in their true light. On the matter of infant baptism, for instance, Mormon invites people to

> listen to the words of Christ, your Redeemer, your Lord and your God. Behold, I came into the world not to call the righteous but sinners to repentance; the whole need no physician, but they that are sick; wherefore, little children are whole, for they are not capable of committing sin; wherefore the curse of Adam is taken from them in me. . . .
>
> For awful is the wickedness to suppose that God saveth one child because of baptism, and the other must perish because he hath no baptism. . . .
>
> He that saith that little children need baptism denieth the mercies of Christ, and setteth at naught the atonement of him and the power of his redemption. (Moroni 8:8, 15, 20)

In Augustinian theology, Adam and Eve failed all humankind by partaking of the fruit and consequently being cast out of Eden. Eve, having been the first to partake and having induced Adam to do so, is thus thought to be culpable for our living in a world of evil and sin. The idea is captured in Lucas Cranach's (1472–1553) painting of Paradise, which hangs in the Kunsthistorisches Museum in Vienna. Cranach, it might be noted, was a confidant of Martin Luther, whom he also painted. In this painting, which is rich both in color and in symbolism, Adam and Eve are standing before the tree of the knowledge of good and evil. A snake with a human head and arms is coiled around the tree. The snake is reaching out to offer the fruit of the tree to our first parents. Close examination reveals that the head of the snake is the mirror image of Eve. The idea being conveyed is that Eve is Satan's accomplice, which notion has given biblical authority to the subjection of the entire female gender.

Latter-day Saint theology differs quite sharply from these negative views of Mother Eve. Indeed, as we shall yet see, it holds her in the highest regard. Let it suffice for the moment to return to her remarkable summation of the gospel of Jesus Christ wherein she said, "Were it not for our transgression we never should have had seed, and never should have known good and evil, and the joy of our redemption, and the eternal life which God giveth unto all the obedient." To this the text adds, "And Adam and Eve blessed the name of God [meaning they offered praise to him], and they made all things known unto their sons and their daughters" (Moses 5:11–12). This is the first recorded testimony of the redemption of Christ uttered by a woman.

Under the heading of the "Fall of Man," Buck's *Theological Dictionary*, held to be the theological standard in Joseph Smith's day, expresses the prevailing view of our first parents thus: "In the fall of man we may observe, 1. The greatest infidelity.—2. Prodigious pride.—3. Horrid ingratitude.—4. Visible contempt of God's majesty and justice.—5. Unaccountable folly.—6. A cruelty to himself and to all his posterity."[3]

Not only does the Augustinian doctrine malign Adam and Eve, but in Catholicism it gave birth to the necessity of the doctrine of Immaculate Conception. Since all men are subject to sin by birth, Christ could not be a son of Adam, that is, he could not descend, as scripture declares, through Abraham, David, and Jesse, for they are sons of Adam and participators in the original sin. To meet the terms of this doctrine Mary had to be conceived immaculately, that is, without the intervention of a father, so that she in turn could conceive a child without a father.

If the proof of a doctrine is, as the Savior said it would be, in the fruits it bears, the Augustinian doctrine of the Fall does not fare well. As we have noted, it dispenses with the justice of God in condemning the unborn child. It does the same with all who have died without hearing the gospel in this life. It relegates women to a lesser role in society, it condemns our first parents, and it creates the need for the concocting of a doctrine that has both Mary and Christ born without a father—hence, he can claim to be the Son of God only in a figurative sense.

Though Augustine's influence was largely limited to the Western church, he dominated medieval, Protestant, and post-Reformation Catholic theology. He is considered by Evangelical Protestants to be the "theological fountainhead" of the Reformation, from which flows their teachings relative to salvation and grace. His concept of fallen man shaped the thinking of Martin Luther and his doctrine of justification by grace, as well as John Calvin's doctrine of election to grace. Calvin held that God preordained some, without any merit of their own, to eternal salvation, and others, in just punishment of their sin, to eternal damnation. The five points of Calvinism are recalled by using the acrostic "TULIP."

T stands for "Total Depravity," in which state man is born. He thus is not only hopelessly sinful, but that sin has extended to all parts of his being, "his thinking, his emotions, and his will."

U stands for "Unconditional Election," representing the fact that all are born into one of two groups: those called or elected to be saved and those who remain to be damned. The choice is God's alone. Those who are saved are saved by his mercy, not by their works; and those who are deserving of damnation so deserve by the very nature of their birth.

L stands for "Limited Atonement," which means that Christ atoned only for the sins of those chosen to be saved.

I stands for "Irresistible Grace," which means that those whom God has called will inevitably come to a knowledge of God.

P stands for "Perseverance of the Saints," which simply means once saved always saved. There is nothing you can do to alter your call to grace.

It is not without significance that we as Latter-day Saints have received by revelation a direct refutation of each of the five points of Calvinism. Consider them in order:

Of *Total Depravity,* the Lord said:

"Every spirit of man was innocent in the beginning; and God having redeemed man from the fall, men became again, in their infant state, innocent before God" (D&C 93:38).

Of *Unconditional Election,* Nephi declared:

For behold, my beloved brethren, I say unto you that the Lord God worketh not in darkness.

He doeth not anything save it be for the benefit of the world; for he loveth the world, even that he layeth down his own life that he may draw all men unto him. Wherefore, he commandeth none that they shall not partake of his salvation.

Behold, doth he cry unto any, saying: Depart from me? Behold, I say unto you, Nay; but he saith: Come unto me all ye ends of the earth, buy milk and honey, without money and without price.

Behold, hath he commanded any that they should depart out of the synagogues, or out of the houses of worship? Behold, I say unto you Nay.

Hath he commanded any that they should not partake of his salvation? Behold I say unto you Nay; but he hath given it free for all men; and he hath commanded his people that they should persuade all men to repentance.

Behold, hath the Lord commanded any that they should not partake of his goodness? Behold I say unto you, Nay; but all men are privileged the one like unto the other, and none are forbidden. . . .

He inviteth them all to come unto him and partake of his goodness; and he denieth none that come unto him, black and white, bond and free, male and female; and he remembereth the heathen; and all are alike unto God, both Jew and Gentile. (2 Nephi 26:23–28, 33)

Of *Limited Atonement*, Jacob, brother to Nephi, said:

It must needs be an infinite atonement. . . .

And he cometh into the world that he may save all men if they will hearken unto his voice; for behold, he suffereth the pains of all men, yea, the pains of every living creature, both men, women, and children, who belong to the family of Adam.

And he suffereth this that the resurrection might pass upon all men, that all might stand before him at the great and judgment day.

And he commandeth all men that they must repent, and be baptized in his name, having perfect faith in the Holy One of Israel, or they cannot be saved in the kingdom of God. (2 Nephi 9:7, 21–23)

Of *Irresistible Grace,* our revelations consistently declare the doctrine of agency:

"Wherefore men are free according to the flesh," stated Father Lehi, "and all things are given them which are expedient unto man. And they are free to choose liberty and eternal life, through the great Mediator of all men, or to choose captivity and death, according to the captivity and power of the devil; for he seeketh that all men might be miserable like unto himself" (2 Nephi 2:27).

> For the power is in them, wherein they are agents unto themselves. And inasmuch as men do good they shall in nowise lose their reward.
>
> But he that doeth not anything until he is commanded, and receiveth a commandment with doubtful heart, and keepeth it with slothfulness, the same is damned.
>
> Who am I that made man, saith the Lord, that will hold him guiltless that obeys not my commandments? (D&C 58:28–30)

Of *Perseverance of the Saints,* the founding document of Mormonism declares:

> And we know also, that sanctification through the grace of our Lord and Savior Jesus Christ is just and true, to all those who love and serve God with all their mights, minds, and strength.
>
> But there is a possibility that man may fall from grace and depart from the living God;

Therefore let the church take heed and pray always, lest they fall into temptation;

Yea, and even let those who are sanctified take heed also. (D&C 20:31–34)

It is profoundly significant that each of the five principles upon which Calvinism is based are directly and emphatically refuted by divine revelation. There is no compromise here. Ours is not a borrowed faith. We stand independent. It is not upon common ground that we have built the house of our understanding.

Our testimony of Christ cannot rest on false principles, nor can it rest on the philosophical speculations of men. It must rest on principles of truth, and all such principles, by their very nature, must come to us by the spirit of revelation. While we may use words in common with those of other faiths in testifying of Christ, we do not share the same meaning. There should be no confusion on this matter. We stand independent of the theological traditions of the rest of Christianity. We bear testimony of principles of light and truth, and they stand in stark distinction with the doctrines and teachings of the churches of the world. The simple and absolute verity is that without a correct understanding of the Fall you cannot, worlds without end, possess a correct understanding of the Atonement.

NOTES

1. Barker, *Apostasy from the Divine Church*, 441; see also Schaff, *History of the Christian Church*, 3:834.
2. See http://history.hanover.edu/texts/trent/ct05.html.
3. Buck, *Theological Dictionary*, 182.

CHAPTER 4

A FALL FORWARD

THE strength of our testimony rests in the light of heaven. Let us now see how that light shines forth from Eden and how it radiates from the man Adam and the woman Eve, earth's first witnesses of Christ and that salvation found only in him. At issue is this: What do the revelations of the Restoration tell us about this story? Do they speak on those matters upon which the Bible is silent? Do they tell us why Adam fell and how his fall effects us?

RESTORING THE DOCTRINE OF AGENCY

Perhaps the first thing that ought capture our attention in a proper telling of the Eden story is the place given in the revelations of the Restoration to the principle of agency. We have already seen how our Heavenly Father made the office and calling of our Redeemer and Savior a matter of agency by asking the question, "Whom shall I send?" Christ's response, "Here am I, send me," was a free-will offering. There was no compulsion. We also saw how Satan "sought to destroy the agency of man" (Moses 4:3). In the Eden story, after the Father had given the charge to Adam not to partake of the tree of knowledge of good and evil, these words are restored to the text: "Nevertheless, thou mayest choose for thyself, for it is given unto thee" (Moses 3:17).

Affirming this principle in a revelation to the Prophet Joseph Smith, the Lord explained that Adam was to be "an agent unto himself." "And it came to pass that Adam, being tempted of the devil—for, behold, the devil was before Adam, for he rebelled against me, saying, Give me thine honor, which is my power; and also a third part of the hosts of heaven turned he away from me because of their agency; and they were thrust down and thus came the devil and his angels. . . . And it must needs be that the devil should tempt the children of men, or they could not be agents unto themselves" (D&C 29:35–39). The whole story centers around agency. We had it in the premortal life, Adam had it in Eden, and it is absolutely essential to the plan of salvation that we have it in this life.

Agency is the power to act, and if we do not become "agents unto ourselves" we cannot work out our salvation. Salvation is not something that God imposes on some and withholds from others, as Augustine and Calvin taught. This is contrary to the very nature of God and the order of heaven. As Christ freely chose to be our Savior, we must freely choose to accept that salvation. So it was with Christ, so it was with Adam, and so it must be with us.

Thus the Lord explained that only if there is agency can we know the bitter from the sweet. If there were no choices, if there was no power granted to us to act upon those choices, we could not know the joy of accomplishment, we would not have the power to give, to bless, or to create, and life would be devoid of all meaning. The Lord explained further:

The devil tempted Adam, and he partook of the forbidden fruit and transgressed the commandment, wherein he became subject to the will of the devil, because he yielded unto temptation.

Wherefore, I, the Lord God, caused that he should be cast out from the Garden of Eden, from my presence, because of his transgression, wherein he became spiritually dead, which is the first death, even that same death which is the last death, which is spiritual, which shall be pronounced upon the wicked when I shall say: Depart, ye cursed.

But, behold, I say unto you that I, the Lord God, gave unto Adam and unto his seed, that they should not die as to the temporal death, until I, the Lord God, should send forth angels to declare unto them repentance and redemption, through faith on the name of mine Only Begotten Son. (D&C 29:40–42)

It is in conjunction with this declaration that the Lord also notes that "little children are redeemed from the foundation of the world through mine Only Begotten" (D&C 29:46).

Now as we begin to see the story unfolding before us, we understand that if life is to have meaning we must have the capacity to act for ourselves; if we are to give freely, we must have agency. If there is no agency, no other gospel principle can exist. If agency is going to exist, then there must be choices to make and the freedom to make them.

Adam Fell to Institute the Plan of Redemption

It is to Father Lehi that we turn to find the key that unlocks the gates of Eden. Having taught that all things exist because they have their opposite, Lehi tells us that the forbidden fruit of

Eden stood in opposition to the tree of life, "the one being sweet and the other bitter."

"Wherefore," he said, "the Lord God gave unto man that he should act for himself. Wherefore, man could not act for himself save it should be that he was enticed by the one or the other."

Lehi then rehearses the story of the first fall, or the devil being cast from heaven. "Because he had fallen from heaven, and had become miserable forever, he sought also the misery of all mankind," Lehi explained. Thus he offered the forbidden fruit to Adam and Eve, who partook and were cast out of Eden.

If Adam had not transgressed, Lehi tells us, "he would have remained in the garden of Eden. And all things which were created must have remained in the same state in which they were after they were created; and they must have remained forever, and had no end" (2 Nephi 2:15–22).

This is a marvelous commentary on the nature of the *Creation*. All things had been pronounced good or godlike; there was no such thing in Eden as death, decay, or corruption in any form. These all belong to the mortal world, of which we are a part, but they are unknown in eternal realms. To place in operation the great plan of redemption, Lehi tells us that "Adam fell that men might be; and men are, that they might have joy" (2 Nephi 2:25; emphasis added).

Here, then, is the key lost to all who have not embraced the spirit of revelation. Adam and Eve had been given conflicting commandments that they might exercise the principle of agency. On the one hand, they had been commanded to multiply and replenish the earth, but they could do so only by partaking of the fruit of the tree of the knowledge of good and evil, which had been forbidden to them. The choice was theirs. They could live forever in a paradisiacal state, but if they did they would remain without children and be unable to grow and progress. On the other hand, they could partake of the fruit, gain the power of procreation, leave the garden, and confront all the vicissitudes of mortal life. In this instance, they and their children through all generations of time would have to trust in Christ for their redemption from the effects of the Fall.

The distance between the Fall and the Atonement in Mormon theology is the distance between the period that ends one sentence and the first word that begins the next. No sooner does Lehi declare that Adam fell than he begins his testimony relative to the coming of Christ:

> And the Messiah cometh in the fulness of time, that he may redeem the children of men from the fall. And because that they are redeemed from the fall they have become free forever, knowing good from evil; to act for themselves and not to be acted upon, save it be by the punishment of the law at the great and last day, according to the commandments which God hath given.
>
> Wherefore, men are free according to the flesh; and all things are given them which are expedient unto man. And they are free to choose liberty and eternal life, through the great Mediator of all men, or to choose captivity and death, according to the captivity and power of the devil; for he seeketh that all men might be miserable like unto himself. (2 Nephi 2:26–27)

At the telling of this story, many have been puzzled as to why God would give commandments that conflict, failing to recognize that this typifies their own lives. We all regularly find ourselves in a position where two or more good things demand our time and attention at the same time. The situation demands a choice, and so we chose between good, better, and best and, like Adam and Eve, live with the consequences of those choices.

DID ADAM REALLY SIN?

Latter-day Saint theology does not hold to the idea that either Adam or Eve "sinned" in partaking of the forbidden fruit. More properly, we speak of Adam's "transgression." For instance the second article of faith reads: "We believe that men will be punished for their own sins, and not for Adam's transgression." Whereas sin consists in willful disobedience, transgression, in this context, centers on a law that was broken. When laws collide but wisdom prevails, we break the lesser to keep the greater. The sin would be in choosing to keep the lesser law at the expense of the greater good.

The law of common sense, for instance, holds that it is not a good idea to jump out of a second-story window. In the case of a fire, this may represent the better part of wisdom. The fact that you are doing the right thing, however, does not excuse you from the consequences of your action. Even though it may be a good idea to jump, it is still going to hurt when you land. So it was with Adam and Eve. They did the right thing but still suffered the consequences.

Many illustrations could be cited in which a commandment of God was of necessity broken in order to keep a higher or greater commandment. In the first chapter of Exodus, we read how the children of Israel were becoming more numerous than the Egyptians. The Egyptian king ordered the Hebrew midwives to kill all the male children. They did not do so. When called to account for their failure they lied to the king, saying that the

Hebrew women were so full of strength that they delivered their own children before they could get there to attend them. We are then told that God blessed the households of the midwives with great posterity for their having so deceived the king.

An untruth was told, and lying does not accord with the gospel standard, but it is most assuredly a minor offense when compared with killing newborn children. We might designate the lie as a transgression for a law was broken, though it was broken in order to keep the greater law, that being to preserve the lives of the male children.

Joseph Smith's Testimony

While in Washington, D.C., in early 1840, Joseph Smith gave a public discourse, a synopsis of which was reported by a correspondent for the *New York Enquirer*. Upon reading the published account of his remarks, the Prophet directed that it be included in his personal history. The article reads in part as follows:

> He [Joseph Smith] commenced by saying, that he knew the prejudices which were abroad in the world against him, but requested us to pay no respect to the rumors which were in circulation respecting him or his doctrines. He was accompanied by three or four of his followers.
>
> He said, "I will state to you our belief, so far as time will permit." "I believe," said he, "that there is a God, possessing all the attributes ascribed to Him by all Christians of all denominations; that He reigns over all things in heaven and on earth, and that all are subject to his power." He then spoke rationally of the attributes of Divinity, such as foreknowledge, mercy &c., &c.

He then took up the Bible. "I believe," said he, "in this sacred volume. In it the 'Mormon' faith is to be found. We teach nothing but what the Bible teaches. We believe nothing, but what is to be found in this book. I believe in the fall of man, as recorded in the Bible; I believe that God foreknew everything, but did not foreordain everything; I deny that foreordain and foreknow is the same thing. *He foreordained the fall of man; but all merciful as He is, He foreordained at the same time, a plan of redemption for all mankind. I believe in the Divinity of Jesus Christ, and that He died for the sins of all men, who in Adam had fallen.'"*

He then entered into some details, the result of which tended to show his total unbelief of what is termed original sin. He believes that it is washed away by the blood of Christ, and that it no longer exists. As a necessary consequence, he believes that we are all born pure and undefiled. That all children dying at an early age (say eight years) not knowing good from evil, were incapable of sinning; and that all such assuredly go to heaven. "I believe," said he, "that a man is a moral, responsible, free agent; that although it was foreordained he should fall, and be redeemed, yet after the redemption it was not foreordained that he should again sin. In the Bible a rule of conduct is laid down for him; in the Old and New Testaments the law by which he is to be governed, may be found. If he violates that law, he is to be punished for the deeds done in the body."[1]

A PROFOUND DIFFERENCE

The restored gospel allows all the children of men the opportunity to be full participants in their own salvation. We have all heard someone say, "I was saved by Jesus two thousand years ago, and there is nothing I can do about it." This would be salvation without agency; it would make us an object to be acted upon while leaving us powerless to choose our own destiny. It makes void the declaration that we were created in the image and likeness of God and robs meaning from every virtue and godly attribute that we might possess. There is no true religion without agency; it gives life and meaning to all things. You can no more compel a man to heaven than you can force someone to love you.

With the knowledge we receive from the revelations of the Restoration, the man Adam and the woman Eve take their rightful place as the honored parents of our race. A healthy understanding of the Fall leaves us with no reason to lament their course in partaking of the forbidden fruit or to demean them on any other count. They walked and talked with God both before and after the Fall, and they bequeathed to us the ability and power to become like unto them and unto their divine parents. In very deed, "Adam fell that men might be; and men are, that they might have joy" (2 Nephi 2:25).

NOTE

1. Smith, *History of the Church,* 4:77–79; emphasis added; paragraphing has been changed.

CHAPTER 5

THE GOODNESS OF OUR GOD

As Latter-day Saints we have all too often attempted to gain a strong and meaningful testimony of Christ without taking the time to lay the proper foundation. We cannot be competent witnesses of Christ without being at the same time competent witnesses of the doctrine of the Fall. Now, let us state more clearly than we have to this point the nature of fallen man. We take the questions the Psalmist asked so long ago as the point of our beginning, "What is man, that thou art mindful of him? and the son of man, that thou visitest him? For thou hast made him a little lower than the angels, and hast crowned him with glory and honour" (Psalm 8:4–5). Modern translators render the word *angels* as "god" and even in some instances as "God." The word *angels* as used in this text is a translation of the Hebrew *elohim,* which indeed means "Gods." The translators' discomfort in allowing man to be thought of as having a divine nature prevented many of them from rendering the text as the Psalmist intended.

At issue here is the nature of man. Is man inherently good or inherently evil? As we have seen, Augustine and his disciples after him, including John Calvin and Martin Luther, thought man to be inherently evil; whereas the revelations given through the Prophet Joseph Smith announce man to be divine by nature. What we are seeking to understand is how the Fall affects the nature of men and women who are the spirit children of divine parents, created in their image and likeness. Just what power is it that Satan gains over man because of man's fallen state? Answering such a question must bring with it a greater appreciation for the nature of the Atonement and our everlasting indebtedness to Christ.

The Effects of the Fall on the Nature of Man

Explaining the principles here involved, Enoch said, "Because that Adam fell, we are; and by his fall came death" (Moses 6:48). Enoch thus tells us that the Fall brought both death and life—that is, the inevitability of death and the power of procreation—to all the family of Adam. As the Book of Mormon repeatedly tells us, death is of two kinds, spiritual and temporal. Temporal death is the separation of the body and the spirit. Spiritual death is to be "shut out from the presence of God" because we have yielded to that which is "carnal, sensual, and devilish" (Moses 6:49). This is the state of "the natural man" who, in the memorable words of King Benjamin, "is an enemy to God, and has been from the fall of Adam, and will be, forever and ever, unless he yields to the enticings of the Holy Spirit, and putteth off the natural man and becometh a saint through the atonement of Christ" (Mosiah 3:19).

Book of Mormon prophets are united in teaching that it is because of the "flesh," meaning blood, that Satan has power over us and that as long as we have blood coursing in our veins, meaning as long as we are subject to death, Satan will have power to tempt us.

Nephi said, "If I do err, even did they err of old; not that I would excuse myself because of other men, but because of the weakness which is in me, *according to the flesh,* I would excuse myself" (1 Nephi 19:6; emphasis added).

Lehi enjoined us to keep the commandments of the Messiah and "not choose eternal death, according to *the will of the flesh and the evil which is therein,* which," he said, "giveth the spirit of the devil power" to take us captive and lead us "down to hell" (2 Nephi 2:29; emphasis added).

In like manner, we remember Nephi's expression of lament, "O wretched man that I am! Yea, my heart sorroweth *because of my flesh;* my soul grieveth because of mine iniquities. I am encompassed about, because of the temptations and the sins which do so easily beset me" (2 Nephi 4:17–18; emphasis added).

Jacob stated the matter thus: "Wherefore, my beloved brethren, reconcile yourselves to the will of God, and not to *the will of the devil and the flesh;* and remember, after ye are reconciled unto God, that it is only in and through the grace of God that ye are saved" (2 Nephi 10:24; emphasis added).

"We are unworthy before thee," the brother of Jared said in prayer. *"Because of the fall our natures have become evil continually"* (Ether 3:2; emphasis added).

By contrast we note with interest the description of translated beings given to us in 3 Nephi. There must be "a change wrought upon their bodies, or else it needs be that they must taste of death." This change resulted in their not being able to suffer pain or sorrow except for the sins of the world. "Now this change was not equal to that which shall take place at the last day; but there was a change wrought upon them, insomuch that Satan could have no power over them, that he could not tempt them; and they were sanctified in the flesh, that they were holy, and that the powers of the earth could not hold them" (3 Nephi 28:37–39).

It is blood that gives death dominion over the physical tabernacle. Immortal beings do not differ from mortals in appearance or nature but rather in the fluid that flows in their veins. "Death had no dominion over his [Adam's] tabernacle: the principle of blood which flows in the mortal tabernacles of men did not exist in his immortal body," explained Orson Pratt, "but his veins and arteries contained a fluid of a far purer nature than that of blood: in other words, they were filled with the spirit of life, which was calculated to preserve them in immortality."[1]

Adam fell from a state of immortality to mortality; that is, he fell from a state in which he, like all other immortal beings, did not have blood in his veins. Blood is the corruptible element in the body; because of it we are subject to sickness, aging, and death; because of it we are subject to the temptations of the devil and are by our nature (to the extent that we have not tamed it) "carnal, sensual, and devilish." As long as we are mortal, we are his subjects in that he can tempt or deceive us. Thus the nature of man, which is inherently good, is subject to that which is inherently bad, and this life will be a battleground for all who come into it, regardless of the circumstances in which they live.

ADAM AND ENOCH TESTIFY OF CHRIST

We find this in the writings of Enoch:

And he called upon our father Adam by his own voice, saying: I am God; I made the world, and men before they were in the flesh.

And he also said unto him: If thou wilt turn unto me, and hearken unto my voice, and believe, and repent of all thy transgressions, and be baptized, even in water, in the name of mine Only Begotten Son, who is full of grace and truth, which is Jesus Christ, the only name which shall be given under heaven, whereby salvation shall come unto the children of men, ye shall receive the gift of the Holy Ghost, asking all things in his name, and whatsoever ye shall ask, it shall be given you.

And our father Adam spake unto the Lord, and said: Why is it that men must repent and be baptized in water? And the Lord said unto Adam: Behold I have forgiven thee thy transgression in the Garden of Eden.

Hence came the saying abroad among the people, that the Son of God hath atoned for original guilt, wherein the sins of the parents cannot be answered upon the heads of the children, for they are whole from the foundation of the world.

And the Lord spake unto Adam, saying: Inasmuch as *thy children are conceived in sin,* even so when they begin to grow up, sin conceiveth in their hearts, and they taste the bitter, that they may know to prize the good. (Moses 6:51–55; emphasis added)

Latter-day Saints cannot read this sentence without quickly adding to the text "thy children were conceived *in a world of sin.*" Our concern is unnecessary. Enoch and Adam are not teaching that it was a sin to conceive children but rather that all children are conceived subject to sin because they are mortal creatures with blood flowing in their veins. Telestial beings, even little children, cannot stand in the presence of God without being translated. It was necessary for Christ himself to be transfigured to stand in the presence of God while he was a mortal man. That which is telestial cannot abide that which is celestial.

Continuing his quotation from Adam, Enoch said:

And it is given unto them [the little children as they grow to maturity] to know good from evil; wherefore they are agents unto themselves, and I have given unto you another law and commandment.

Wherefore teach it unto your children, that all men, everywhere, must repent, or they can in nowise inherit the kingdom of God, for no unclean thing can dwell there, or dwell in his presence; for, in the language of Adam, Man of Holiness is his name, and the name of his Only Begotten is the Son of Man, even Jesus Christ, a righteous Judge, who shall come in the meridian of time.

Therefore I give unto you a commandment, to teach these things freely unto your children, saying:

That by reason of transgression cometh the fall, which fall bringeth death, and inasmuch as ye were born into the world by water, and blood, and the spirit, which I have made, and so became of dust a living soul, even so ye must be born again into the kingdom of heaven, of water, and of the Spirit, and be cleansed by blood, even the blood of mine Only Begotten; that ye might be sanctified from all sin, and enjoy the words of eternal life in this world, and eternal life in the world to come, even immortal glory (Moses 6:56–59).

ANGELS TO A DEVIL

No prophet has taught the doctrine of the Atonement with greater power and force than Jacob, the son of Lehi. It is generally understood that the Atonement made resurrection possible. Jacob addresses the question as to what would have happened if no atoning sacrifice had been made. "If the flesh should rise no more," he says, "our spirits must become subject to that angel who fell from before the presence of the Eternal God, and became the devil, to rise no more. And our spirits must have become like unto him, and we become devils, angels to a devil, to be shut out from the presence of our God, and to remain with the father of lies, in misery, like unto himself" (2 Nephi 9:8–9).

Had there been no Atonement made, every descendant of Adam would at death be perdition. We would become citizens of the kingdom of the devil. Tainted with sin, we would be in bondage to the father of sin in a kingdom from which there could be no deliverance. Lucifer would be our king, and we would be his subjects. In his kingdom there is neither freedom nor agency; we would be powerless to do anything other than worship him. Such would be our fate throughout the endless expanses of eternity.

Having brought us to this stark realization, Jacob bursts forth in praise: "O how great the goodness of our God, who prepareth a way for our escape from the grasp of this awful monster; yea, that monster, death and hell, which I call the death of the body, and also the death of the spirit." Jacob defines the separation of body and spirit as the temporal death and the separation of the spirit from the presence of God as spiritual death. It is because of the Atonement of Christ that all who have died will be made alive again, both those in hell and those in paradise (see 2 Nephi 9:10–15).

THE NATURE OF MAN

Having considered key revelations dealing with the nature of man and his complete dependency on the grace of God for salvation, we conclude as follows. First, all children of God were born into this life pure, clean, innocent, and holy (see D&C 93:38). Further, we believe that "the Son of God hath atoned for original guilt, wherein the sins of the parents cannot be answered upon the heads of the children" (Moses 6:54). Thus, as our article of faith states: "We believe that men will be punished for their own sins, and not for Adam's transgression" (Articles of Faith 1:2).

At the same time, we believe that a *natural birth creates a natural man,* meaning that as long as we have blood flowing in our veins we are in some measure subject to the power and influence of the adversary. As long as we live and as long as we are in a probationary state, we are subject to temptation and will be called upon to resist and fight against the appetites of the flesh.

The often-asked question relative to the nature of man is not really the relevant issue, but rather the issue is the power Satan has over the flesh, or over us in this mortal state. We were born divine in nature, created both as spirits and in physical form in the image and likeness of God. Satan is at war with all that comes from God and thus seeks our destruction. In this life he has power over us because of our flesh, meaning because we have blood coursing in our veins, and thus are corruptible. Adam and Eve were not created with blood in their veins.

So it is that we must be born again, which is to put off the natural man by yielding to the enticing of the Holy Spirit, becoming "as a child, submissive, meek, humble, patient, full of love" and "willing to submit to all things" that mortal life may inflict upon us (Mosiah 3:19), yet imbued with that faith that will enable us to rise above all that is ungodly (see D&C 76:53).

Without the Fall There Is No Need for an Atonement

Some years ago I spent some hours in conversation with a Jewish rabbi. I asked him what his expectations relative to a Savior were. "I have no need of a Savior," he responded. It was then that

I realized that without an understanding of the Fall, there can be no understanding of the need for a Redeemer. It is not an uncommon thing for missionaries to meet someone who asks them how they could possibly be expected to believe in God "if . . ." and then the "if" is followed by some sorrowful thing like the death of their spouse or a little child or the hunger or suffering that exists somewhere in our fallen world. While the reality of the Fall is generally understood in the traditional Christian world, there is no clear understanding of its nature. This in turn means that there can be no clear understanding of the nature of the Atonement.

As we have seen in this chapter, the Book of Mormon prophets had a clear understanding of this matter. They write with plainness about the fact that Adam fell from a state in which he had no blood to one in which he did. Indeed, we might say that it was a blood fall that necessitated a blood atonement. From their teachings we learn that as long as we have blood we are subject to death and suffering. As long as we have blood we will grow old and die. As long as we have blood we can get sick and suffer. As long as we have blood, Satan has some degree of power over us.

They also teach us that as death (blood) came upon us all because of the Fall of Adam, God in his goodness and justice responded through Christ in the form of a resurrection that will inseparably unite body and spirit everlastingly together. They also assure us that all who so chose through their faith and obedience to accept and follow Christ will be granted eternal life, meaning that they will inherit the endless joy known only to exalted beings. Jacob tells us that if it had not been for Christ and his atoning sacrifice, the victory would have gone to Satan, and we—and all created things—would have remained subject to him through the endless eternities, which is to say that we would have become devils or angels to a devil (perdition) forever.

This knowledge gives us greater reason to rejoice in that which Christ did for us.

This additional understanding brings with it an additional power to our testimony. Add then to this the knowledge that through Christ's Atonement we can eventually receive a fulness of all that the Father has, and again our testimony reaches far beyond that of those who cannot even imagine such a thing. And thus it is that we find ourselves embracing Jacob's refrain, "O how great the goodness of our God" (2 Nephi 9:10).

NOTE

1.   Pratt, *Journal of Discourses*, 7:254.

CHAPTER 6

THE SECRETS OF EDEN

A s already noted, the revelations of the Restoration give us the key by which we unlock the gates of Eden, that we might enter and learn all that is to be found there that pertains to our salvation and the testimony we have been commissioned to bear of Christ. Let us now seek so to do.

FIGURATIVE OR LITERAL

The first great question we must ask is if we are to understand the Eden story figuratively or literally.

The name Adam comes from the common Hebrew word for man or mankind. In the Eden story, the point at which *adam* should be rendered as a proper name is not agreed upon. The Hebrew word for *woman* can also be translated "wife." Many religious writers and teachers look upon the story as an allegory in which Adam and Eve represent humankind. The story, it is held, is simply a way for the primitive mind of man to give expression to the origin of their species. This allows religion to accommodate the theories of science.

For instance, *The Oxford Dictionary of the Christian Church* states: "In modern times the whole concept of the Fall has often been rejected as inconsistent with the facts of man's development known to science, esp. with evolution. *The Biblical story itself belongs to the realm of myth.* . . . The Church has seen in the story of Gen. 2 f. a fundamental truth about man in his relation to God, even if the truth is held to be there conveyed in legendary form."[1]

Declaring the story of Eden to be a myth, regardless of how many other difficulties of faith it solves for some, creates a greater problem for all. You cannot poison the roots of a tree without destroying the fruit, and if it is the tree of life you poison, it is the fruits of everlasting life that you destroy. The matter is simple: if Adam is a myth—that is, if there was no man Adam but he was as so many declare him to be, a mythical representation of man's origins—then the Fall is also a myth; and if the Fall is a myth, then the Atonement that comes in answer to the Fall is a myth; and if the Atonement is a myth, then Christ is a myth; and thus with the innocence of myth we have completely destroyed any hope we might have of an answer to the fallen state of man and of the hope of life after death.

Moroni taught the principle with perfect succinctness saying: "Behold, he [God] created Adam, and by Adam came the fall of man. And because of the fall of man came Jesus Christ, even the Father and the Son; and because of Jesus Christ came the redemption of man" (Mormon 9:12).

Question: Would this then mean that everything within the story must be understood as being literally so? For instance, are we to suppose that Adam was created from the dust of the earth, Eve from his rib, and that Eve did indeed have a conversation with a snake?

Answer: No, it is not water that washes away our sins, but repentance and our act of contrition and respect for the authority of the priesthood. It is not the oil that heals in the administration of the sick but the outpouring of the Spirit which it represents; and the bread and water that we partake of in the sacrament are not literally the flesh and blood of Christ but a plain and simple symbol of his infinite and eternal sacrifice in our behalf. Adam was not made of dust or clay or even red earth. He is as the heaven-sent word declares him to be, "the son of God" (Moses 6:22), the "firstborn" of mortal men (Abraham 1:3), "the direct and lineal offspring of Deity,"[2] who with Eve, his wife, was created "in the image and likeness of God" (Genesis 1:26–27). Dust is the symbol for that which is mortal and the rib a symbol not for the creative act but for the place of the woman everlastingly at the side of her husband, not a step before him or a step behind him but "bone of [his] bones, and flesh of [his] flesh (Genesis 2:23).

"Man, in his fulness, is a twofold organization—male and female. Either being incapable of filling the measure of their creation alone, it requires the union of the two to complete man in the image of God, for in Gen. 1:27, it expressly says, that he was created male and female in the image of God. Therefore, without the proper union of the sexes, man would be less than what God created him."[3]

And as for conversations with animals, readers may choose whether they want to believe that or not, but in either case the snake represented Satan, which is beyond debate.

Symbols clothe ideas in beauty and power. They speak with greater depth and meaning than do words. The story of Eden as preserved for us in scripture draws heavily on language and images, the meaning of which have become lost to most of us because our culture has so little time and interest in learning these things. Below is a review of key phrases from the story of Eden. You will find possible explanations given to various phrases which are of importance in properly understanding the meaning and significance of a great scriptural story, which in turn was intended to help us unlock and understand all that follows in the history of Israel.

Behold, it was very good (Genesis 1:31)	*Perfect in their kind; Godlike*
The dust of the ground (Genesis 2:7)	*The manner of birth known to all humankind*
The breath of life (Genesis 2:7)	*The immortal spirit entering the body*
A garden eastward in Eden (Genesis 2:8)	*Variously known as the holy garden, mountain of God, or the temple*
The tree of life (Genesis 2:9)	*Jesus the Christ*
The tree of knowledge of good and evil (Genesis 2:9)	*Its fruits, both bitter and sweet, represent the culmination of man's experience*
In the day that thou eatest thereof (Genesis 2:17)	*A day with the Lord is a thousand years with man*
[From Adam's rib] made he a woman (Genesis 2:22)	*Represents the proper place of the woman, at the side of man*
Bone of my bones, and flesh of my flesh (Genesis 2:23)	*The oneness of the woman with the man*

And they shall be one flesh (Genesis 2:24)	*Sexual union*
The serpent (Genesis 3:1)	*The devil*
Your eyes shall be opened (Genesis 3:5)	*Your understanding shall increase; your mind shall be enlightened*
They were naked (Genesis 3:7)	*The innocence of a child*
They sewed fig leaves together (Genesis 3:7)	*The fig is a symbol of fertility; by partaking of the fruit they obtained the power of procreation*
And made themselves aprons (Genesis 3:7)	*They had now become a tree of life*
Thorns and thistles (Genesis 3:18)	*Including grievances and difficulties*
Dust thou art, and unto dust shalt thou return (Genesis 3:19)	*The mortal body will return to the element from which it was made*
God made coats of skins and clothed them (Genesis 3:21)	*The promise of protection in and through the blood of the Lamb; the Atonement will rectify all the effects of Adam's Fall*

Cherubims, and a flaming sword (Genesis 3:24)	*Fallen man, all that is unclean, cannot enter the presence of the Lord; thus sentinels guard the way*
Called their name Adam (Genesis 5:2)	*Eve took Adam's name, symbolizing her oneness with him*

The story of Eden is told in symbolic language. This, however, does not justify the idea that the story is a myth. Again, no Adam, no Fall; no Fall, no Atonement; no Atonement, no Christ; no Christ, no plan of salvation and no hope. There is room for differences of opinion in the interpretation of the story. For instance, some hold that it was the eating of actual fruit that caused blood to course in the veins of Adam and Eve; others believe that the story of the fruit is simply a symbolic representation of some law or combination of laws that they broke to create blood in their bodies. This is of little consequence. What is of particular moment here is that Adam and Eve fell from a state in which they did not have blood to one in which they did. Because it was a blood fall, it required a blood atonement; because the Fall inflicted mortality, the Atonement of necessity must restore immortality.

THE THREE PILLARS OF ETERNITY

Elder Bruce R. McConkie coined the phrase the "three pillars of eternity" in describing the inseparable nature of the Creation, the Fall, and the Atonement.[4] In telling that story, he noted for us that it was essential to understand that all things were created in a state of immortality; that is, they were not subject to death or corruption of any sort, nor was procreation possible to them. These are fruits of mortality, and so in partaking of the fruit Adam and Eve brought death not only to themselves but also to all other living things. The earth and all life upon it became subject to death by the command of Adam's priesthood, and so it would be that the act of redemption must restore all things to their primeval state. The missing part of this triune of principles in the book of Genesis is the clear statement of the necessity of the Atonement to come in answer to the Fall, and this is precisely what is restored to the account in the Book of Moses.

In the Book of Moses, no sooner are Adam and Eve cast out of the Garden of Eden than we read that God commanded them to practice the law of sacrifice as it had been taught to them in the Garden. The command was that they offer "the firstlings of their flocks, for an offering unto the Lord," to which command they were obedient.

> And after many days an angel of the Lord appeared unto Adam, saying: Why dost thou offer sacrifices unto the Lord? And Adam said unto him: I know not, save the Lord commanded me.
>
> And then the angel spake, saying: This thing is a similitude of the sacrifice of the Only Begotten of the Father, which is full of grace and truth.
>
> Wherefore, thou shalt do all that thou doest in the name of the Son, and thou shalt repent and call upon God in the name of the Son forevermore.
>
> And in that day the Holy Ghost fell upon Adam, which beareth record of the Father and the Son, saying: I am the Only Begotten of the Father from the beginning, henceforth and forever, that as thou hast fallen thou mayest be redeemed, and all mankind, even as many as will. (Moses 5:6–9)

This restoration of text is most profound. It restores Christ to the Old Testament and to the testimony and faith of all the faithful people of the Old Testament. It means that Adam was the first Christian, the first to be baptized in the name of Christ and the first to bear witness and testimony of him, and that Eve was the second. If there is a power of salvation in the Christian message, then Adam and Eve had it. It means that the gospel did not evolve any more than God evolved or man evolved. It means that we look to Adam and Eve as two great witnesses of Christ rather than two weak, pathetic characters who inflicted evil upon all mankind through their incontinence.

Eden As a Temple Metaphor

Should it ever be our privilege to call upon Father Adam and ask him to share with us his treasured memories of Eden, can we not confidently suppose that he would speak in reverent terms of walking with God and being instructed by him? Would he not speak of hands that were laid upon his head to convey the priesthood and its keys to him as Joseph Smith told us had happened? Would he not tell of his marriage with his beloved companion, Eve, and the charge given to them to multiply and fill the earth with their posterity? Would he not recount the instruction given him and his eternal companion, by which they could obtain the fulness of heavenly knowledge and power? Would he not rehearse how he had been taught the law of sacrifice (see Moses 5:4–8) and how he and Eve had been clothed in the garments of salvation preparatory to their entering the lone and dreary world, where they were to be tried and tested in all things?

A rehearsal of the key events in Eden brings the realization that we too are privileged to leave the world and enter the sacred sanctuaries of the Lord, where we participate in essentially the same experiences known to our first parents before the Fall. The temple is to us as Eden was to Adam and Eve. It is in the temple that we, like Adam and Eve, are invited to walk with God; it is in the temple that we are instructed in those things that we must do to return to his holy presence; it is in the temple that we are married for eternity and commanded to multiply and replenish the earth; it is within these sacred walls that we are taught the law of sacrifice, placed under covenant to be true and faithful, and clothed in a garment of protection.

After Adam and Eve had partaken of the forbidden fruit, but before they were expelled from the Garden, the Father taught them the law of sacrifice. Animals were slain that Adam and Eve might be clothed in "coats of skins" (Moses 4:27). Thus the sacred clothing given them in Eden was to serve as a constant reminder that through the atoning blood of Christ they would be protected from all the effects of the fallen world into which they would now enter. Through his blood they could obtain a remission of sins, be born again, and return to the divine presence.

Adam and Eve were further instructed by an angel of the Lord that they were to take upon them the name of Christ and that all they did was to be done in his name (see Moses 5:8). Thus as God had clothed them in coats or garments of skin as a token of the protection provided them through Christ—protection from the effects of a fallen world—so they were to clothe themselves in his name by faith, and in that name they were to do all that they did that pertained to salvation or to things of the Spirit. Thus they were assured that they could overcome all things.

"He that hath an ear, let him hear," John wrote unto the seven churches in Asia, "what the Spirit saith unto the churches; To him that overcometh will I give to eat of the tree of life" (Revelation 2:7). The fruit is the gospel of Jesus Christ and is described by Lehi as being "desirable to make one happy" and as filling the soul with "exceedingly great joy" (1 Nephi 8:10, 12). To Nephi it was revealed that the tree of life—that tree which stood in the midst of Eden—represented the love of God, and by extension, the eternal life made possible by the Atonement of his Son (see 1 Nephi 11:4–23).

THE BLESSINGS OF ETERNAL LIFE

Through their Eden experience Adam and Eve instituted the plan of salvation both for themselves and for their posterity, and so it is that we too institute that plan in our lives and in behalf of our posterity through the ordinances of the temple. Thus it was that by partaking of the fruit of the tree of life Adam and Eve became

> as Gods, knowing good from evil, placing themselves in a state to act, or being placed in a state to act according to their wills and pleasures, whether to do evil or to do good—
>
> Therefore God gave unto them commandments, after having made known unto them the plan of redemption, that they should not do evil, the penalty thereof being a second death, which was an everlasting death as to things pertaining unto righteousness; for on such the plan of redemption could have no power, for the works of justice could not be destroyed, according to the supreme goodness of God.
>
> But God did call on men, in the name of his Son, (this being the plan of redemption which was laid) saying: If ye will repent, and harden not your hearts, then will I have mercy upon you, through mine Only Begotten

Son; therefore, whosoever repenteth, and hardeneth not his heart, he shall have claim on mercy through mine Only Begotten Son, unto a remission of his sins; and these shall enter into my rest.

And whosoever will harden his heart and will do iniquity, behold, I swear in my wrath that he shall not enter into my rest. (Alma 12:31–35)

So it is that the revelations of the Restoration exonerate Adam and Eve, give meaning and purpose to both the creation story and the story of the Fall, and show us that all that has taken place from the beginning is by divine plan, the plan of redemption or the plan of happiness. The story is an eloquent testimony that Joseph Smith is, indeed, a prophet of God and the great revelator of Christ, for this the greatest of all gospel dispensations.

NOTES

1. *Oxford Dictionary of the Christian Church*, 501; emphasis added.
2. First Presidency, "The Origin of Man," 4:206.
3. Richards and Little, *Compendium of the Doctrines of the Gospel*, 117.
4. McConkie, "The Three Pillars of Eternity."

CHAPTER 7

THE ORDINANCES
TESTIFY OF CHRIST

O UR participation in the ordinances of the gospel is an expression of our testimony of Christ. The ordinances in turn enlarge our testimony of the Savior, for each of them bring knowledge and understanding that we could not otherwise have. This is simply a case of testimony begetting testimony. Such is the divine system. As the truths of heaven are revealed to us line upon line, so the ordinances of the gospel lead one to another, each revealing truths that prepare us for that which is to follow. Thus we advance from grace to grace until we receive a fulness of truth and understanding. So it is that no binding testimony of Christ can stand independent of obedience to the laws and ordinances of the gospel. To deny the ordinances and the authority by which they are performed is to deny Christ, who instituted them.

A REVELATION TO THOSE OF OTHER FAITHS

Suppose that, as a missionary, you and your companion were out knocking on doors and were invited in by a man who then told you that he had been a Baptist minister for forty years. Let us then suppose that you take the occasion to bear your testimony to him of a God who speaks, of modern revelation, and of living prophets. Being a good, honest man, he is impressed with your message and asks what God would say if he were to speak to him. What might be of special interest to you is that this very thing happened in the day of Joseph Smith and that the Prophet sought a revelation for this man, whose name was James Covill. Now, what is it that you would expect the Lord to say to him? Here is what he said: "He that receiveth my gospel receiveth me; and he that receiveth not my gospel receiveth not me. [The reference here is to the restored gospel.] And this is my gospel—repentance and baptism by water, and then cometh the baptism of fire and the Holy Ghost, even the Comforter, which showeth all things, and teacheth the peaceable things of the kingdom" (D&C 39:5–6).

To accept Christ is to accept his gospel, and that gospel is and always has been centered in our participating in ordinances. To reject the ordinances is to reject Christ. Thus the Lord told James Covill to "arise and be baptized, and wash away your sins, calling on my name, and you shall receive my Spirit, and a blessing so great as you never have known. And if thou do this, I have prepared thee for a greater work. Thou shalt preach the fulness of my gospel, which I have sent forth in these last days, *the covenant* which I have sent forth to recover my people, which are of the house of Israel" (D&C 39:10–11; emphasis added).

The Lord credits James Covill with having done a good work in that he was preparing people to accept the fulness of the gospel when it came to them, and the Lord tells him that he can do a vastly greater work through accepting that fulness, being baptized, and then teaching the message of the covenant to others.

The phrase "the covenant" is the key part of this text. The Lord's people have always been a covenant people, and that covenant begins with the ordinance of baptism.

In a revelation penned two months later, the Lord said:

Hearken, O ye people of my church, and ye elders listen together, and hear my voice while it is called today, and harden not your hearts; for verily I say unto you that I am Alpha and Omega, the beginning and the end, the light and the life of the world—a light that shineth in darkness and the darkness comprehendeth it not.

I came unto mine own, and mine own received me not; but unto as many as received me gave I power to do many miracles, and to become the sons of God; and even unto them that believed on my name gave I power to obtain eternal life.

And *even so I have sent mine everlasting covenant into the world, to be a light to the world, and to be a standard for my people, and for the Gentiles to seek to it, and to be a messenger before my face to prepare the way before me.* (D&C 45:6–9; emphasis added).

Later that same year, 1831, the Lord gave a revelation explaining why he organized his Church again upon the earth. Four reasons are given: first, "that every man might speak in the name of God the Lord, even the Savior of the world [that is, hold the priesthood]"; second, "that faith also might increase in the earth"; third, "*that mine everlasting covenant might be established*"; and fourth, "that the fulness of my gospel might be proclaimed by the weak and the simple unto the ends of the world" (D&C 1:20–23; emphasis added).

The Law of Sacrifice

The law of sacrifice, as we have already seen, was instituted by God in Eden as a similitude of the atoning sacrifice of the Lamb of God wherein Adam, Eve, and all their posterity might be reconciled to God. Its introduction in Eden constitutes the first messianic prophecy and immediately follows the partaking of the forbidden fruit, or the Fall of Adam. Jacob, son of Lehi, tells that his people kept records that their children in future generations would look with joy and not with sorrow, neither with contempt, concerning their first parents.

> For, for this intent have we written these things, that they may know that we knew of Christ, and we had a hope of his glory many hundred years before his coming; and not only we ourselves had a hope of his glory, but also all the holy prophets which were before us.
>
> Behold, they believed in Christ and worshiped the Father in his name, and also we worship the Father in his name. And for this intent we keep the law of Moses, it pointing our souls to him; and for this cause it is sanctified unto us for righteousness, even as it was accounted unto Abraham in the wilderness to be obedient unto the commands of God in offering up his son Isaac, which is a similitude of God and his Only Begotten Son. (Jacob 4:4–5)

The Law of Circumcision

From Abraham to Christ, circumcision was the token of the covenant God made with the house of Israel by which the blessings of salvation were to flow to them (see Genesis 17). From the Joseph Smith Translation, we learn the circumstances that called forth the renewal of this covenant that had first been made with Adam and Eve: "My people have gone astray from my precepts, and have not kept mine ordinances, which I gave unto their fathers," the Lord said, "and they have not observed mine anointing, and the burial, or baptism wherewith I commanded them; but have turned from the commandment, and taken unto themselves the washing of children, and the blood of sprinkling; and have said that the blood of the righteous Abel was shed for sins; and have not known wherein they are accountable before me."

To correct this state of apostasy, the Lord said,

And I will establish a covenant of circumcision with thee, and it shall be my covenant between me and thee, and thy seed after thee, in their generations; that thou mayest know for ever that children are not accountable before me until they are eight years old.

And thou shalt observe to keep all my covenants wherein I covenanted with thy fathers; and thou shalt keep the commandments which I have given thee with mine own mouth, and I will be a God unto thee and thy seed after thee. (JST, Genesis 17:11–12; Bible appendix)

BAPTISM OF WATER AND OF THE SPIRIT

No other gospel ordinance is as obviously Christ centered as the ordinance of baptism. Teaching the symbolism of baptism, the Apostle Paul wrote:

Know ye not, that so many of us as were baptized into Jesus Christ were baptized into his death?

Therefore we are buried with him by baptism into death: that like as Christ was raised up from the dead by the glory of the Father, even so we also should walk in newness of life.

For if we have been planted together in the likeness of his death, we shall be also in the likeness of his resurrection:

Knowing this, that our old man is crucified with him, that the body of sin might be destroyed, that henceforth we should not serve sin. (Romans 6:3–6).

To this the revelations of the Restoration add:

1. That baptism in the name of Christ was had from the days of Adam and has always been practiced by the Lord's people (see Moses 6:52).
2. That proper priesthood authority is necessary in the performance of this ordinance (see D&C 13, 22).
3. The words of the baptismal prayer and that the one performing the ordinance is to completely immerse the one being baptized in water and bring him or her forth again (see D&C 20:72–74).
4. That baptism of little children is mockery before God and a denial of Christ's atoning sacrifice (see Moroni 8:9–20).
5. That the proper age to qualify to be baptized is eight years of age (see D&C 68:25; JST, Genesis 17:11).
6. That vicarious baptisms for our kindred dead who did not have the opportunity to be baptized while in the flesh are to be performed by the proper authority

in temples of the Lord, built and dedicated for that purpose (see D&C 124:29–39).

7. That baptism of water is but half a baptism and worth nothing without the other half, which is receiving the Holy Ghost (see D&C 20:38–43).

8. That the covenant of baptism is the ordinance to which scattered Israel must be gathered (see D&C 39:10–11; 137:6).

"TO FULFILL ALL RIGHTEOUSNESS"

Matthew recounts for us how Jesus walked from Galilee to Jordan to be baptized by John his cousin. Knowing that Jesus was the promised Messiah and the Son of God, John was hesitant to baptize him. Jesus brought an immediate end to John's hesitancy saying, "Suffer it to be so now: for thus it becometh us to fulfil all righteousness" (Matthew 3:15).

At this point in the story we begin a careful consideration of the word *righteousness*. It is a translation of the Greek *dikaios*, which means "just." That which is righteous is that which is just, meaning justified or approved by God. For instance, to say that a man is "justified by faith" (Romans 5:1; Galatians 3:24) is to say that his course has been approved by God; that is, that he has complied with the divine law. So what Christ was saying to John, in effect, was, "You must baptize me or my course will not be approved by God, nor will yours either, for the responsibility and authority to baptize rests with you."

It is at this point that Nephi picks up the story and unfolds it to us. "If the Lamb of God, he being holy," he reasons, "should have need to be baptized by water to fulfil all righteousness, O then, how much more need have we, being unholy, to be baptized, yea, even by water!" (2 Nephi 31:5).

Is it possible, we ask, for someone to be "holy" and yet not "righteous"? To which we answer, Yes. A little child is holy, meaning without sin, but is incapable of righteousness, which requires conscious action on his or her part. Christ was without sin, and he had been set apart to the service of the Lord, but he could not be considered righteous or justified until he complied with the law.

Then Nephi gives us five reasons why Christ was baptized: (1) to show his subservience or humility to the Father (see 2 Nephi 31:7); (2) to accord with his covenant to do the will of the Father in keeping all his commandments (see v. 7); (3) to show the straitness of the path that leads to the presence of the Father, which in effect is to say that he too had to enter in at the gate or remain outside the kingdom of God (see v. 9); (4) to set an example for everyone else who sought entrance into the kingdom (see v. 9–10); (5) to receive the gift of the Holy Ghost (see v. 8). Nephi tells us that after Christ was baptized, the Holy Ghost descended upon him.

The gift of the Holy Ghost is given only to those who have been baptized. Nephi explained, "The voice of the Son came unto me, saying: He that is baptized in my name, to him will the Father give the Holy Ghost, *like unto me;* wherefore, follow me, and do the things which ye have seen me do" (2 Nephi 31:12; emphasis added). As Christ needed baptism to enter the kingdom of God, so he needed the gift of the Holy Ghost that he might speak and act by the spirit of revelation; such are the divine laws given to the children of men.

In a marvelous messianic prophecy, Malachi described the promised Messiah as the "messenger of the covenant" (Malachi 3:1). Because the prophecy extends to our day—and to ensure that we would be familiar with it—Christ quoted it as part of his covenant discourse in 3 Nephi 24. The finest scriptural commentary on this phrase is found in Nephi's explanation (above) of why Christ was baptized. Nephi gives us an entirely different perspective of Christ and his ministry than that professed by modern Christendom. This is a perfect illustration of the new witness of Christ found in the Book of Mormon.

The Ordinance of the Sacrament

The ordinance of sacrament and the manner in which it centers our attention on Christ and his atoning sacrifice in our behalf needs little commentary. The sacrament is understood to be a renewal of the covenants made when we were baptized (see D&C 20:77). It is the system by which we regularly receive a remission of sins, by covenant, to move forward in the service and cause of Christ, especially the keeping of the covenants we have made.

Honoring the Priesthood

To hold the priesthood is to have been commissioned to act as an agent for God. The call to function in such a manner can come only from God and must accord with the procedures he has established to identify those called to represent him. When the foundation of the Church was laid, the Lord said, "It shall not be given to any one to go forth to preach my gospel, or to build up my church, except he be ordained by some one who has authority, and it is known to the church that he has authority and has been regularly ordained by the heads of the church" (D&C 42:11).

"Wherefore, let all men beware how they take my name in their lips—for behold, verily I say, that many there be who are under this condemnation, who use the name of the Lord, and use it in vain, having not authority" (D&C 63:61–62).

That is to say, unless God speaks to us, we cannot speak for him. There can be no salvation without revelation. It is also to say that the "priesthood administereth the gospel" and that the ordinances of the priesthood are essential to salvation (see D&C 84:19). The terms of salvation are not determined by popular vote or by an elect and selective group of men. Salvation is the gift of God and is his alone to give. Salvation comes on his terms and his alone. God does not and cannot honor promises given without his authority, nor can he reward even the best of efforts made in the service of false principles or a false god. Truth alone has the power of salvation in it, and all the truths of salvation have two characteristics in common: they come from God by revelation, and they will be confirmed through the ordinances of the priesthood, without which we have no claim to them in the world to come (see D&C 132:7–13).

The full and proper name of the Melchizedek Priesthood is the Holy Priesthood after the Order of the Son of God (see D&C 107:3). It comes to us, according to the words of Alma, in such a manner as to teach us how to look to the Son of God for redemption (see Alma 13:2). Alma speaks particularly of the office of high priesthood, noting in effect that all high priests are types and shadows of Christ, for as he was called and prepared before the foundations of the earth were laid, so were they. As he was ordained in the councils of heaven to teach the gospel of salvation, so were they.

All that we do by the power and authority of the priesthood constitutes our testimony of Christ. To accept and live in accordance with those ordinances is essential in making us competent witnesses of Christ.

CHAPTER 8

MAN OF HOLINESS

You cannot have true religion without a correct understanding of the nature of God. If you believe God to be a spirit essence without form or substance and stand to testify that Jesus Christ is his Son, just what does that mean? Surely, we could not conclude that Christ's claim to divine Sonship is to be taken literally and that Christ is the son of God in the same sense that you and I are sons or daughters of our parents. The nature of the God in which you believe shapes the nature and meaning of every doctrine that comes from him. If God were to declare himself to be incomprehensible, then surely we would err in the attempt to understand him. For us then to stand and announce anything relative to such a God with certainly would make us false witnesses, for he had explicitly told us that such knowledge could not be ours. If we suppose that the God of the Old Testament was a God of vengeance while the God of the New Testament was a merciful and loving God, would we not be left to wonder how many Gods there were and whether they were gracious or vengeful?

If we adopt the idea that God does not have "body, parts, or passions," that he is not a corporeal being, then though we read a thousand times over in scripture the references that assert otherwise, we would be obligated to call them metaphors and explain them away by saying that they were given to aid those of simple mind in understanding what little they can. If we then declare this to be a fundamental principle of salvation, we have at the same time declared that all who read scripture without our prior instruction relative to what is and what is not to be believed would have no chance of arriving at the truth on their own. Such a course would preclude any real trust in our own ability to understand the meaning of scripture without the aid of someone to predetermine its meaning for us. If this were the case, personal scriptural study could prove to be very perilous and should be discouraged. This would place the priest or minister entrusted with the word between us and the God of heaven. We could commune with the heavens only through him.

What we have just described is the traditional Christian world as it exists today. To this mass of confusion let us then add this observation: everyone is reading scripture according to a preconceived conception what they think it should be saying. No one comes to the reading of any book without preconceptions of some sort. All too often scripture is read not in the search for truth but in search for evidence that what someone has predetermined can be sustained as truth. Choosing what we will accept as scripture, what we will accept in the scripture, and how we will accept it constitutes a marvelous test of our spiritual integrity.

THE LATTER-DAY SAINT GOD

The Latter-day Saint concept of God centers in and grows out of our faith in the Bible as the word of God and the idea that people can be trusted to read it by themselves. We begin the telling of our story with Joseph Smith's reading of James 1:5, wherein he found the invitation for all who lacked wisdom to ask God directly for it. He desired to know which of all the churches he should join. In response to his humble and heartfelt question, the heavens were opened and "two Personages" appeared before him, standing above him in the air. One of them addressed him by name saying, "[Joseph,] This is My Beloved Son. Hear Him!" (JS–H 1:17).

With that story commences a great flood of knowledge relative to God and his designs for the salvation of his children. As we recount the doctrines of great importance to be learned from this experience, we begin with the verity that God speaks. The fact that he does so today confirms our faith that he did so anciently. God stands revealed or remains forever unknown. He chose to be known and manifested himself to Joseph Smith.

Many have been quick to point out a biblical text that states, "No man hath seen God at any time" (John 1:18). Thus, they contend, our story certainly could not be in harmony with the Bible. The text is an odd one, for it stands in opposition to a significant number of instances in the Bible wherein God did indeed manifest himself to men. We will set that consideration aside for the moment. Let it simply be observed that the statement that no one had to that point done something does not preclude someone in the future from doing it. In Joseph Smith's day, no one had flown in an airplane. Today many people have. Our testimony is that Joseph Smith did indeed see both the Father and the Son. It is a testimony born of the spirit of revelation, as that spirit rests in all who bear it. He was thus earth's most competent witness as to their existence and their nature.

From that experience we learn that they were "Personages" with all the form of men, they were separate and distinct, and they had no reluctance to speak to and instruct the youthful Joseph Smith. They had chosen him to reveal their nature to those of every nation, kindred, tongue, and people.

Without belaboring the detail of each revelation, let us note some of the great scriptural and doctrinal statements we have from Joseph Smith about these heavenly beings. We ought to first note, however, that one of the greatest lessons learned by Joseph Smith in this sublime experience was that the hundreds upon hundreds of references in the Bible to a God who is a corporeal being were intended to mean precisely what they say, as are the scores of references describing the appearance of God to men.

It is a matter of great interest as to how much mischief or unbelief can result from a single sentence that has obviously been mistranslated. Conversely, it is remarkable how much light and truth can be restored in one or two sentences. Consider this illustration from the Book of Moses:

> Now this prophecy Adam spake, as he was moved upon by the Holy Ghost, and a genealogy was kept of the children of God. And this was the book of the generations of Adam, saying: In the day that God created man, in the likeness of God made he him;
>
> In the image of his own body, male and female, created he them, and blessed them, and called their name Adam, in the day when they were created and became living souls in the land upon the footstool of God. (Moses 6:8–9)

Note the following:
1. Adam is a prophet. He speaks by way of prophecy.
2. Adam had the gift of the Holy Ghost.
3. Adam had a written language.
4. God considered Adam's children to be his children.
5. Both Adam and his children were created in the image of God's body. Let it be shouted from the housetops:

not only is God a being of form and substance, but he has "a body" like that had by the children of Adam.

6. Eve bore her husband's name, undoubtedly as a symbol of the perfect unity and oneness that was to exist between them.

Later in the same chapter of Moses, Enoch, who is teaching the doctrine of the Fall, says, "Teach it unto your children, that all men, everywhere, must repent, or they can in nowise inherit the kingdom of God, for no unclean thing can dwell there, or dwell in his presence; for, in the language of Adam, Man of Holiness is his name, and the name of his Only Begotten is the Son of Man, even Jesus Christ" (Moses 6:57).

What is the name-title Enoch gives to the great Elohim, the Father of us all? It is "Man of Holiness," that it might be known forever that God the Eternal Father is an exalted, resurrected, glorified, and perfected man. The whole system and plan of salvation grows out of this sublime truth. "In the pure language spoken by Adam—and which will be spoken again during the millennial era (Zeph. 3:9)—the name of God the Father is *Ahman*, or possibly *Ah Man*, a name-title having a meaning identical with or at least very closely akin to *Man of Holiness* (Moses 6:57). God revealed himself to Adam by this name to signify that he is a *Holy Man*, a truth which man must know and comprehend if he is to become like God and inherit exaltation."[1]

We have it from Orson Pratt that

there is one revelation that this people are not generally acquainted with. I think it has never been published, but probably it will be in the Church History. It is given in questions and answers. The first question is, "What is the name of God in the pure language?" The answer says,

"Ahman" "What is the name of the Son of God?" Answer, "Son Ahman—the greatest of all the parts of God excepting Ahman." "What is the name of men?" "Sons Ahman," is the answer. "What is the name of angels in the pure language?" "Anglo-man."[2]

Part of this revelation is preserved for us in Doctrine and Covenants 78:20, in which we are told that Christ is "the Son Ahman."

The Book of Mormon is an eloquent witness that the spirit prior to birth has the same form and likeness that it will have when it is clothed in flesh and that the body is retained in the resurrection in the same likeness. The premortal Christ appeared to the brother of Jared, saying: "Seest thou that ye are created after mine own image? Yea, even all men were created in the beginning after mine own image. Behold, this body, which ye now behold, is the body of my spirit; and man have I created after the body of my spirit; and even as I appear unto thee to be in the spirit will I appear unto my people in the flesh" (Ether 3:15–16).

When the resurrected Christ appeared to the Nephites we are told that the Father introduced him from the heavens, saying, "Behold my Beloved Son, in whom I am well pleased, in whom I have glorified my name—hear ye him. And it came to pass, as they understood they cast their eyes up again towards heaven; and behold, they saw a Man descending out of heaven; and he was clothed in a white robe; and he came down and stood in the midst of them" (3 Nephi 11:7–8).

In Doctrine and Covenants 130:22, we read, "The Father has a body of flesh and bones as tangible as man's; the Son also; but the Holy Ghost has not a body of flesh and bones, but is a personage of Spirit. Were it not so, the Holy Ghost could not dwell in us."

A few weeks before his death, the Prophet Joseph Smith put

a seal or crown upon the doctrines he had taught in a discourse given to honor a dear friend, King Follett, who was accidentally killed while digging a well in Nauvoo. On that occasion the Prophet said:

> God himself was once as we are now, and is an exalted man, and sits enthroned in yonder heavens! That is the great secret. If the veil were rent today, and the great God who holds this world in its orbit, and who upholds all worlds and all things by his power, was to make himself visible,—I say, if you were to see him today, you would see him like a man in form—like yourselves in all the person, image, and very form as a man; for Adam was created in the very fashion, image, and likeness of God, and received instruction from, and walked, talked and conversed with him, as one man talks and communes with another.[3]

THE GOD WE WORSHIP

The testimony we bear to all the world is that God is a loving father and that we are actually and literally created in his image and likeness. He is the father of our spirits, and we rightfully and properly speak of him as our Father in Heaven. He is father to the physical tabernacle of Adam and Eve, who we are told were "in the image of his own body" (Moses 6:9). He is an exalted, resurrected, glorified Man and has instituted a plan for our salvation that centers in the divine invitation for each of us to return to his presence as his rightful heirs to possess the fulness of all that he has and thus be "equal in power, and in might, and in dominion" with him (D&C 76:95).

These truths have been known to all who faithfully followed his prophets in past dispensations. Yet all of these truths have been lost to traditional Christianity. Today they are unique and distinctive to The Church of Jesus Christ of Latter-day Saints. They constitute the reason we have been commissioned to go to those of every nation, kindred, tongue, and people to declare the restored gospel. We seek to take back to them those truths that were lost from among them. Our commission is to all people in all places because these truths were lost to all people in all places.

In countless instances, our missionaries have been asked why they come to disturb good Christian people in their faithful worship. It is because they are good Christian people that we come. It is because of the love of the Lord that they profess that we knock on their doors and respectfully ask to speak to them. Our message is that they are loved of God and that he designs and desires to share greater light and truth with them. He would have them know that he is the very God spoken of in those scriptures they reverence and that once we restore to them the key of knowledge they will read those scriptures with new eyes and see them with new understanding. We bring to them a reunion with the feelings of their hearts and the principles that were planted there long before they were born.

How often it is that missionaries teach some principle distinctive to the restored gospel only to have those they teach say, "I always believed that!"—and of course they did? It is knowledge they brought with them into this life, and hearing it is like seeing an old friend for whom there is an immediate moment of recognition. It is always awkward in such instances to point out that the truths involved are not taught in the churches to which they belong. Often those being taught stubbornly insist that they are, for where else could they have come to know them? Again the answer rests with the restored gospel, which alone can explain how we are born with a distant memory that enables us to recognize light and truth when it is returned to us.

One thing that is especially important here is to see how quickly these lights can be turned out. All that God has restored to us can be lost in a single generation if we are careless in the manner in which we pass the torch to those destined to follow us. The distortion of a single principle can result in the loss and understanding of all principles. By simply denying form and substance to God, in the simple act of robbing him of his body, you destroy the entire plan of salvation. We cannot rob God of his body without surrendering our own kinship with him. Thus we lose the knowledge of our own divine capacity and suppose ourselves to be the descendants of animals or that we were created out of nothing; we lose the knowledge of the resurrection and the purpose of the Atonement. Quickly and silently the doctrines fall, one after another, until we are left with nothing but a shadow of what we once had.

It is common for missionaries to have someone say to them, "Well, it is all the same God, isn't it?" Our answer to such a statement must be an emphatic and yet gracious, "No." If it is all the same God, why were Joseph and Hyrum killed in the Carthage Jail? Why were our forebears driven from New York to Missouri, and from Missouri to Illinois, and from Illinois to a territory outside the boundaries of the United States? Why have so many Latter-day Saints been disowned by their families when they joined the Church?

Notes

1. McConkie, *Mormon Doctrine,* 29.
2. Pratt, in *Journal of Discourses,* 2:342.
3. Smith, *Teachings,* 345.

CHAPTER 9

THE SON OF MAN

O UR testimony of Christ centers on the verity that he is actually and literally the Son of God. We testify— and the whole plan of salvation rests on this truth— that God is the father of Christ and that they are as separate and distinct as every soul born in this world is separate and distinct from their own parents. For us the name *father* is not a metaphor but carries the plain meaning of the word; he is the "male parent" of Christ. When we say Christ is the Son of God, we are not speaking in figurative language; we mean that he is the male offspring of God the Father and Mary of Nazareth. We believe him to be the Only Begotten of the Father in the flesh. That is to say, we believe that Jesus, the son of Mary of Nazareth, was the only son God ever sired who had a mortal mother. We believe that we are all spirit sons and daughters of God, born as such long before those spirits assumed a tabernacle of flesh, but Christ was the only child who had a mortal mother and who had God as his father.

The LDS Bible Dictionary states the matter thus: "Adam is spoken of as the 'first flesh' upon the earth, meaning he was the first mortal on the earth, all things being created in a nonmortal condition, and becoming mortal through the fall of Adam. Jesus is the 'Only Begotten of the Father' in the flesh, meaning he is the only one begotten of the Father into mortality."[1]

President Ezra Taft Benson taught: "The Church of Jesus Christ of Latter-day Saints proclaims that Jesus Christ is the Son of God in the most literal sense. The body in which He performed His mission in the flesh was sired by that same Holy Being we worship as God, our Eternal Father. Jesus was not the son of Joseph, nor was He begotten by the Holy Ghost. He is the Son of the Eternal Father."[2]

In the book *Mormon Doctrine,* Elder Bruce R. McConkie testifies to this principle in this manner: "God the Father is a perfected, glorified, holy Man, an immortal Personage. And Christ was born into the world as the literal Son of this Holy Being; he was born in the same personal, real, and literal sense that any mortal son is born to a mortal father. There is nothing figurative about his paternity; he was begotten, conceived and born in the normal and natural course of events, for he is the Son of God, and that designation means what it says. (1 Ne. 11.)"[3]

Our Testimony Is in Opposition to the Creeds of Christianity

Latter-day Saints need to clearly understand that it is because we believe that Jesus Christ is actually and literally the Son of God that we are rejected by the traditional Christian world as non-Christian. The creeds of Christendom which give birth to their doctrine of the Holy Trinity do not accord with such an idea. These creedal statements, which are difficult for even their most sympathetic adherents to explain, view the nature of God as a mystery not to be comprehended by mortal men. They do not permit the idea that God is a personal being with body, parts, and passions, nor do they permit the idea that Jesus Christ is a separate personage from the Father and that he was in some way actually the son of the Father. Our testimony of Christ stands in opposition to the creeds, and the creeds stand in opposition to our testimony of Christ. There is no middle ground here.

We may use terms in common with those whose testimony and doctrines are founded on the creeds, but the meaning behind those words is entirely different. If indeed Christianity is to be defined by adherence to the creeds of modern Christendom, then we as Latter-day Saints are clearly not Christians. If the test of Christianity is to believe that Jesus Christ is the Son of God, then we are the most Christian of all Christians. Succinctly stated, our testimony is that Jesus of Nazareth is the Son of God, from whom he inherited immortality, and that he is the son of Mary, from whom he inherited blood or mortality. Thus he was the only man ever to walk the earth who had within himself the capacity to lay down his life and to take it up again (see John 10:18).

DEFINING CHRISTIANITY

There has to be at least a tad of irony in those who profess a love for the Bible telling Latter-day Saints that they are not Christians. No scriptural definition can be given for the word. For them to make such an accusation, then, requires a revelation beyond that found in the Bible, an idea very much at odds with their profession of faith. We have no evidence that God ever used the word *Christian*; thus, the manner in which we choose to use it is, when all has been said and done, simply a measure of our Christianity.

As Latter-day Saints, we hold to the idea that it is for people individually to choose for themselves whether they want to be considered Christian or not. We have no argument with their choice. We do think it strange, however, to have people whose behavior often falls far short of anything of which Christ could be said to approve tell us that we are not Christians. It also seems strange that we are excluded from the community of Christianity because we believe that Christ is actually the Son of God by those who have concluded otherwise through what they themselves admit are not scriptural sources.

THE TESTIMONY OF THE REVELATIONS
OF THE RESTORATION

No book of scripture teaches the doctrine of divine Sonship with greater eloquence than the Book of Mormon. It begins with the testimony of Nephi relative to Christ as the tree of life. Nephi, as the reader will recall, was caught up into an "exceedingly high mountain," phraseology we have come to recognize as the heavenly temple. Here he is interviewed by an angel, who asks if he believes in the tree which his father Lehi saw in vision, which vision Nephi desires to see also. Nephi responds in the affirmative, whereupon the angel cries out, "Hosanna to the Lord, the most high God." The angel then tells Nephi that he can be shown the vision because he believes "in the Son of the most high God."

Nephi is then shown a vision of "a virgin" more beautiful and fair than any other virgin (1 Nephi 11:13). Nephi is asked by the angel if he understands the doctrine of the "condescension of God" (v. 16). He indicates that he does not, whereupon he is told that the virgin whom he saw "is the mother of the Son of God, after the manner of the flesh" (v. 18).

"I beheld," he said, "that she was carried away in the Spirit; and after she had been carried away in the Spirit for the space of a time the angel spake unto me saying: Look! And I looked and beheld the virgin again, bearing a child in her arms. And the angel said unto me: Behold the Lamb of God, yea, even the Son of the Eternal Father!" (vv. 19–21).

Thus we are invited to learn with Nephi, through his experience, that Christ, the tree of life, was God's Son "after the manner of the flesh," all of which was the result of the "condescension" of the Father to do something that Gods simply do not normally do. In the endless expanses of eternity, we know of only one occasion when an exalted being condescended to enter the sacred union of parenthood with a mortal being. This occurred so that Christ would have the unique inheritance described in the preceding verses—he had a God as his Father and a mortal woman as his mother and thus would be able to lay down his life and take it up again, a power that required one parent to be immortal and the other to be mortal. Thus, as with every other soul ever born upon the earth, Christ had both a father and a mother and received a combined inheritance from both. The idea that God, an exalted, glorified man, was involved in the process of Christ's birth is simply not to be found in the creeds of Christendom.

Later in the Book of Mormon, Alma takes up the imagery of Christ being the tree of life and shows that all true faith in Christ is appended to this doctrine. To comply with the law of witnesses, Alma cites three scriptural texts, all known to his readers, in which the coming of God's Son was spoken of. He first quotes a psalm of praise to God, written by Zenos. It praises the Father for the mercy that had come unto him "because of thy Son" (Alma 33:11). Alma then quotes from the writing of Zenock, who said, "Thou art angry, O Lord, with this people, because they will not understand thy mercies which thou hast bestowed upon them because of thy Son" (Alma 33:16). And finally he cites Moses and his raising up the brazen serpent on the pole (see Alma 33:19). Though the full account is not contained in what Alma gives us of this story, it too must have contained reference to Christ as the Son of God. Concluding his discourse Alma says, "And now, my brethren, I desire that ye shall plant this word [that is, the doctrine of divine Sonship] in your hearts, and as it beginneth to swell even so nourish it by your faith. And behold, it will become a tree, springing up in you unto everlasting life. And then may God grant unto you that your burdens may be light, through the joy of his Son" (Alma 33:23).

The scriptural phrase chosen to repetitiously remind us of the doctrine of divine Sonship of Christ is "Only Begotten," used in reference to Christ. It should be noted that this phrase has been removed from modern translations of the Bible, both Catholic and Protestant. In its stead we now read "only Son" or "one and only Son." What is involved here is the translation of the Greek word *monogenes*. When faced with this word, the translator is left with the responsibility to determine if the writer was attempting to tell us that this was the only child of a particular parent, or that this was a child, as it is presently reasoned, who was totally unique. A literal translation conveys the idea that Christ is actually the Son of God—but given that this notion is contrary to the creeds, it has been changed.

In contrast to this, Nephi, Jacob, and Alma all use the phrase "Only Begotten" or "Only Begotten Son" (2 Nephi 25:12; Jacob 4:5; Alma 13:5). The phrase is consistently found in the revelations in the Doctrine and Covenants, and Joseph Smith restored the phrase to the Old Testament, as found in the Book of Moses: "And it came to pass that the Lord spake unto Moses, saying: Behold, I reveal unto you concerning this heaven, and this earth; write the words which I speak. I am the Beginning and the End, the Almighty God; by mine Only Begotten I created these things; yea, in the beginning I created the heaven, and the earth upon which thou standest" (Moses 2:1).

There are about seventy instances in the New Testament where Christ is called the "Son of man." In a number of these texts he applies the term to himself. Those lacking the spirit of inspiration have interpreted this to mean that he is Joseph's son and that he never claimed to be the sire of God. The Joseph Smith Translation consistently changes these texts to read "Son of Man," which accords with an earlier emendation to that text that tells us that the name of the Father is "Man of Holiness" (Moses 6:57). Thus, to say that Christ is the "Son of Man" is to testify that he is actually and literally God's Son.

A classic illustration of this change is found in the conversation recorded in Matthew 16, where Christ asked the Twelve who the people they met and taught thought him to be. He began the discussion asking, "Whom do men say that I, the Son of Man, am?" (JST, Matthew 16:14). They reported a variety of answers, which both separately and collectively evidence that the people generally were expecting a restoration of the gospel at the hands of ancient prophets. Some said that he was John the Baptist, others that he was Elijah, others that he was Jeremiah, or another of the old prophets (see Luke 9:18–19).

Christ then asked the Apostles who they thought him to be. Simon Peter, acting as their spokesman, said, "Thou art the Christ, the Son of the living God" (Matthew 16:16). Christ commended Peter not only for knowing who he was but for getting his testimony by the spirit of revelation. He then told the Apostles that the revelation that he is the Son of God is the bedrock upon which the Church will be founded. It is in this setting that Christ promised Peter that he will yet hold the keys of the kingdom (see Matthew 16:17–19).

It is not sufficient for us to testify that Jesus is the Christ; our testimony must embrace the verity that he is the Son of God. This is the key that unlocks the revelations of heaven to us, as it did for Peter. Another classic illustration of this principle comes from Nephi, in his explanation of how his father unlocked the heavens to receive the revelation that Nephi then sought to obtain. "He spake," Nephi said, "by the power of the Holy Ghost, *which power he received by faith on the Son of God—and the Son of God was the Messiah who should come"* (1 Nephi 10:17; emphasis added).

CONCLUSION

All true religion is based on the testimony that Jesus Christ, the promised Messiah, is actually and literally the Son of God. This doctrine is the key that unlocks the right to revelation and the meaning of all the revelations of heaven. Let it then be noted that the Latter-day Saint testimony of Christ embraces his literal kinship with the Father and that this doctrine gives birth to the doctrine of the Atonement, and the doctrine of the Atonement is the doctrine that gives birth to all other doctrines of salvation. Such is our testimony.

NOTES

1. Bible Dictionary, 675–76.
2. Benson, *Come Unto Christ*, 4.
3. McConkie, *Mormon Doctrine*, 742; emphasis added.

CHAPTER 10

ALL WILL HEAR THE GOSPEL

NOTHING torments traditional Christianity like the question, "What becomes of those who die without the opportunity to hear and accept the gospel of Christ?" or the obvious attendant question, "What becomes of the infant child who dies without confessing the Master?" While many in the Christian world argue that the Bible is sufficient, containing all we need to know about Christ, they find no answer in that holy book to these questions.

Many sincere Christians in our day earnestly seek better answers to such questions than those they have inherited from generations past. While serving as a mission president, I had two men of another faith pay me a visit to assure me that I, as a Latter-day Saint, was hopelessly lost because I had not accepted their version of salvation. I suggested to them that they were faced with a very serious problem. "What?" they asked in a very defiant tone. I responded that more people had died that very day than there were members of their church. "What of them?" I asked. Virtually every one of them had died without hearing their brand of Christianity. "Well," said the spokesman for the two, in a spirit of disgust, "that's their tough luck, isn't it?"

This is not the God of whom we as Latter-day Saints bear witness. Anyone who has tasted the sweetness of the restored gospel will have a hard time imagining how someone can profess faith in such a capricious and unjust God. If the very spirit of Christianity is marked by our concern for others exceeding our preoccupation with ourselves, then how, in the name of Christ, do we overlook the injustice of condemning billions of souls to some sort of eternal punishment for not having accepted a message that was never presented to them?

GIVING BETTER ANSWERS

Once again the understanding we have of this matter traces to the revelations of the Restoration. It was not until January 21, 1836, that Joseph Smith first learned the principle of salvation for the dead. It was imperative that the Church be firmly founded on gospel principles before this principle be revealed to them. No one who has the opportunity to accept and live the gospel in this life can be justified in deferring that responsibility until the next life. Ours is a "day of this life" religion, a "do it now" religion, not a religion in which one can procrastinate the day of his or her repentance.

On the occasion of this revelation, the heavens were opened to Joseph Smith in a magnificent vision in which he saw the Father and the Son seated on the throne of heaven; and he saw Father Adam, Abraham, his own father and mother, and his brother Alvin, who had died in 1823. The Prophet's father and mother were both alive at the time of this vision. In fact, his father was in the room with him, seated at his side. He passed away in 1841, and Joseph's mother lived until 1855. So when

Joseph saw his parents in this vision, he knew that he was seeing things in heaven as they would yet be, not as they then were.

Nevertheless, he was still surprised to see his brother Alvin in the vision, because he had died in 1823, some six years before the authority to baptize was restored by John the Baptist, and he had not been baptized for the remission of sins. The voice of the Lord then spoke, saying: "All who have died without a knowledge of this gospel, who would have received it if they had been permitted to tarry, shall be heirs of the celestial kingdom of God; also all that shall die henceforth without a knowledge of it, who would have received it with all their hearts, shall be heirs of that kingdom; for I, the Lord, will judge all men according to their works, according to the desire of their hearts" (D&C 137:7–9).

The revelation does not justify the idea that there will be a wholesale granting of the gospel to those in the spirit world. It specifically states that the privilege of embracing the gospel and obtaining the blessings of exaltation are exclusively granted to those who: (1) died without the opportunity to hear it in this life; (2) in God's judgment would have accepted it in this life if the opportunity had come to them to do so; and (3) in God's judgment are such that they would have embraced it with "all their hearts," meaning that they would have endured in faith to the end. All who receive the gospel in the spirit world receive it at the same cost in faith, courage, and effort as was required of the living.

Thus we have Peter saying that they would be judged according to men in the flesh, meaning that the gospel and the faith necessary to accept it are the same in both worlds (see 1 Peter 4:6). This greatly expands the meaning of the Prophet's statement in the third article of faith, wherein he said, "We believe that through the Atonement of Christ, all mankind may be saved, by obedience to the laws and ordinances of the Gospel."

When the Prophet said, "all mankind," he meant precisely that: "all mankind," or as we would say today, "all humankind." No one who was ever born into this world will be left without the opportunity to accept or reject the gospel before the day of their resurrection and judgment.

It was not until 1841 that the ordinance of baptism for the dead was revealed to Joseph Smith. As one would expect, his first thought upon receiving this revelation was that Alvin needed to be baptized, which, of course, was immediately done. The reason that Alvin had been shown to the Prophet in the revelation announcing that the gospel was to be taught to those in the spirit world is that he is a perfect example of someone who died without receiving the gospel in this life but who would receive it with all his or her heart as soon as the opportunity was presented in the spirit world.

As I have written elsewhere,

The truths thus revealed must have been the source of great rejoicing in the Smith family. The passing of Alvin had been a matter of considerable sorrow. Their wounded souls had been cut to the core by the unfeeling and intemperate remarks of the Presbyterian minister who had consigned Alvin to hell at his funeral simply because he had not been baptized or involved in that church.

Despite his relative youth, Alvin was a man of unusual spiritual propensity. Before his death, he called each of his brothers and sisters in turn to his bedside and gave them a parting admonition. To his eighteen-year-old-brother Joseph he said: "Be a good boy, and do everything that lies in your power to obtain the Record [the Book of Mormon]. Be faithful in receiving instruction, and in keeping every commandment that is given you." Mother Smith stated that "Alvin manifested, if such could be the case, greater zeal and anxiety in regard to the Record that had been shown to Joseph, than any of the rest of the family; in consequence of which we could not bear to hear anything said upon the subject. Whenever Joseph spoke of the Record, it would immediately bring Alvin to our minds, with all his zeal, and with all his kindness; and, when we looked to his place, and realized that he was gone from it, to return no more in this life, we all with one accord wept over our irretrievable loss, and 'we could not be comforted because he was not.'"

Nearly twenty years later, Joseph Smith recounted his feelings at the time of Alvin's death, saying: "I remember well the pangs of sorrow that swelled my youthful bosom and almost burst my tender heart when he died. He was the oldest and noblest of my father's family. . . . He was one of the soberest of men, and when he died the angel of the Lord visited him in his last moments.[1]

THE VISION OF THE REDEMPTION OF THE DEAD

On October 3, 1918, President Joseph F. Smith, sixth President of the Church, received what is known today as the vision of the redemption of the dead. From this revelation we learn that while Christ's body lay in the borrowed tomb of Joseph of Arimathaea his spirit went, as do the spirits of all humankind, to the world of the spirits, where there awaited him an innumerable host of spirits who had embraced the gospel while in this life and endured in faith to the end. To this assembled host, he taught the principles of the resurrection and the redemption of humankind from the Fall of Adam, on condition of repentance.

We are specifically told that he did not personally administer among the wicked but rather that "from among the righteous, he organized his forces and appointed messengers, clothed with power and authority, and commissioned them to go forth and carry the light of the gospel to them that were in darkness, even to all the spirits of men; and thus was the gospel preached to the dead. . . . Thus was the gospel preached to those who had died in their sins, without a knowledge of the truth, or in transgression, having rejected the prophets" (D&C 138:30, 32).

Those receiving the gospel for the second time would of course be blessed by it but would be confined to the terrestrial kingdom (D&C 76:73–74). All were taught faith in God, repentance from sin, vicarious baptism for the remission of sins, the gift of the Holy Ghost by the laying on of hands, and all other principles of the gospel that were necessary for them to know in order to qualify themselves that they might be judged according to men in the flesh, but live according to God in the spirit" (D&C 138:33–34).

So it was that the preaching of the gospel began in the spirit world, with spirits teaching kindred spirits as we do here in the flesh, and so it has been ever since that time. Thus it is our testimony to all the world that God, in his mercy and justice, will grant every soul who ever drew a breath of air upon this earth the opportunity to have the gospel taught to them, along with the opportunity to exercise their agency in accepting or rejecting it. We further believe that those of that world can, through the exercise of faith in Christ and repentance from their sins, prepare themselves to receive all the ordinances of the house of the Lord, which we will perform in their behalf in our temples. Those for whom these ordinances are performed may accept or reject them, just as they would have accepted or rejected them in this life had the opportunity been theirs.

COMMUNICATING THESE TRUTHS

These truths are well understood among Latter-day Saints and form an important part of our testimony. We express our testimony of these principles each time we go to the temple to involve ourselves in laboring for our kindred dead and in the countless hours that are spent in family research to find the names of those who went before us. In fact, these things are so much a part of our faith—and the evidence of them is so obvious to us, even from Bible texts—that sometimes we assume they must be known at least in part to those of other faiths. They are not. Often we find ourselves using a vocabulary in common with others, only to discover that we have an entirely different understanding of the words being used.

We know resurrection to be the inseparable reunion of the body and spirit. We learn this from the Book of Mormon (see Alma 11:45). The Bible does not define resurrection, and for the most part the Bible-believing world does not believe in a corporeal resurrection. Because this singular truth is lost to the Bible, the idea of a spirit world where spirits await the day of resurrection is also lost to them. If you have no comprehension of the spirit world as a place of temporary residence for the spirit while we await the day of resurrection, you cannot understand the idea of the gospel being taught there. If you do not understand the nature of spirits—that is, for instance, that they are in the likeness of our body—but rather think of them as some formless essence, you will find it difficult to conceive of them teaching each other the gospel. As an understanding of one gospel truth always makes it easier to understand another, so in like manner do errors compound, pushing the truth further and further from us.

To be without these principles is also to be without a God of mercy and justice. This problem has caused many in the traditional Christian world to seek ways to extend the hope of salvation to those to whom their theology affords no such opportunity. In doing this they have been forced to compromise the principles of salvation, saying that they for some reason do not apply to everyone in the world or that there are ways people can obtain salvation independent of Christ. Thus Christ's role as Savior becomes a shared one, and the plan of salvation as announced in the scriptures, which they declared sealed, bears a host of man-made amendments.

It is a sacred privilege to have the truths that have been revealed to us and to be able to bear witness and testimony of them.

NOTE

1.   Millet and McConkie, *The Life Beyond,* 40–41.

CHAPTER 11

RESURRECTION AND ETERNAL MARRIAGE

THE whole gospel plan rises or falls with the doctrine of resurrection. Paul stated it well when he said, If there be no resurrection of the dead, then is Christ not risen: and if Christ be not risen, then is our preaching vain, and your faith is also vain. Yea, and we are found false witnesses of God; because we have testified of God that he raised up Christ: whom he raised not up, if so be that the dead rise not. For if the dead rise not, then is not Christ raised: and if Christ be not raised, your faith is vain; ye are yet in your sins. Then they also which are fallen asleep in Christ are perished. If in this life only we have hope in Christ, we are of all men most miserable" (1 Corinthians 15:13–19).

The resurrection of Christ is the confirming evidence of his divine Sonship and of the truthfulness of the gospel which he taught. It is the single greatest event in earth's history. It confirms his victory over death and the efficacy of his atoning sacrifice. It affirms his position as our Redeemer and Savior and places all humankind in a position wherein they must conform to the laws and ordinances of his gospel if they are to obtain eternal life. It means that there is no other name under heaven whereby men can be saved.

As we discussed in the previous chapter, many struggle to find a way whereby salvation can be extended to the great masses of men who will die without the knowledge of Christ in this life. Whatever that source of that salvation may be, it must have within it the power to call them forth from the grave in a state of immortality, or the argument falls like an autumn leaf from the tree. All such arguments must surrender to the verity that salvation rests with Christ alone, for he alone had the power to overcome death.

Defining Resurrection

No better evidence could be given for the necessity of revelation in our day than the simple fact that a definition of resurrection is lost to the texts that have been preserved for us in the Bible. You may read the Bible from now until doomsday, and from Genesis to Revelation, but you will not find within its covers an explanation of the nature of resurrected beings. It is often suggested that resurrection is the rising of the dead to a state of life. Five such cases are mentioned in the New Testament:

1. The daughter of Jairus (Luke 8:49–55)
2. The widow's son at Nain (Luke 7:11–15)
3. Lazarus of Bethany (John 11:43–44)
4. Dorcas, or Tabitha (Acts 9:36–42)
5. Eutychus (Acts 20:9–12)

Notwithstanding their miraculous return to life, they all died again. Resurrection must be more than reuniting body and spirit. It is as the revelations of the Restoration tell us; it is the "inseparable union" of body and spirit, never again to be divided.

Consider the teachings of Amulek: "I have spoken unto you concerning the death of the mortal body, and also concerning the resurrection of the mortal body. I say unto you that this mortal body is raised to an immortal body, that is from death, even from the first death unto life, that they can die no more; their spirits uniting with their bodies, never to be divided; thus the whole becoming spiritual and immortal, that they can no more see corruption" (Alma 11:45).

Of those who had departed this life, President Joseph F. Smith said, "Their sleeping dust was to be restored unto its perfect frame, bone to his bone, and the sinews and the flesh upon them, the spirit and the body to be united never again to be divided, that they might receive a fulness of joy" (D&C 138:17).

Had the equivalent of either of these two statements been preserved in the Bible as we now have it, a great deal of confusion could have been avoided.

In his definition Amulek tells us that those who are resurrected will have "spiritual" bodies. This should not be confused with a "spirit" body. As used in this context, the word "spiritual" means not subject to death or not corruptible. Moses told us that prior to the Fall, while Adam and Eve lived in Eden, their bodies were "spiritual," again meaning that they were not subject to aging, decay, or corruption of any kind (see Moses 3:5, 7, 9), or as Lehi stated it, they would have "remained [forever] in the same state in which they . . . were created" (2 Nephi 2:22). In the great revelation of resurrection for our dispensation, Joseph Smith was told that those who come forth in the first or celestial resurrection will have "a spiritual body," again meaning that they will not be subject to corruption (see D&C 88:27–28). The Apostle Paul used this phrase in the same manner in his discourse to the Corinthian Saints (see 1 Corinthians 15:44). His statement has caused endless confusion, not because he misspoke but because his readers do not have the understanding of the word that we get from the writings of Moses, Amulek, Lehi, and Joseph Smith. It is from this misunderstanding of what Paul is saying that so many in the traditional Christian world believe that the resurrected body will not be a physical body but only some form of spirit.

Marriage in Heaven

Our missionaries are commonly challenged with the same questions that were asked of Christ during his ministry. One of these deals with the issue of who a particular woman who had been married to seven men would be married to in the resurrection. In response, Christ said, "For in the resurrection they neither marry, nor are given in marriage, but are as the angels of God in heaven" (Matthew 22:30).

It is often extrapolated from Christ's response that there will be no marriages in the resurrection. A more thoughtful look at the verses involved is instructive. The question is asked in the form of a challenge, in the hope of embarrassing Christ. The issue, however, is not marriage; it is resurrection. The Sadducees who have rejected the hope of a resurrection are asking the question. The reason for this is that they find nothing to sustain the idea of resurrection in the scriptures they accept, which are limited to the first five books of Moses. The fact of the matter is that the word *resurrection* does not even appear in the Old Testament, and this story constitutes the first time the word *resurrection* is used in the New Testament.

Christ responds to the question by reminding his questioners that even the scriptures accepted by the Sadducees quote God as saying, "I am the God of Abraham, and the God of Isaac, and the God of Jacob. God is not the God of the dead," he said, "but of the living" (Matthew 22:32–33). The idea is that if he is still the God of Abraham, Isaac, and Jacob, those patriarchs must still be living, even if they have passed from this earth. His questioners were silenced by his answer.

For our purpose, let us go back a step. The story reflects the tradition in ancient Israel that if a man died not having seed, his brothers were required to take his widow as a wife and raise up seed in his name. The continuation of seed was obviously a matter of great importance to their understanding of the gospel. The importance of the continuation of seed was closely related to a second tradition, that marriage and families were to be eternal. It was out of that understanding that this question was born.

In answering this particular question, Christ simply noted that in the case of these Sadducees, who had refused the new baptism he brought and the gospel he taught, there would be no continuation of seed or marriage in the world to come. There is nothing in his response, however, that suggests that eternal marriage would not be available to those who accepted him and complied with the ordinances of salvation. Indeed, such a concept stood at the very heart of the Abrahamic covenant.

The Nature and Appearance of Spirits

It will be recalled that when Christ appeared in the upper room following his resurrection, those there assembled (including his mother, brothers, eleven of the Twelve, and their wives and children) were alarmed, supposing that they were seeing a spirit. This tells us what they understood a man's spirit to look like, which obviously was like they had appeared in mortality. To calm their fears, Christ said, "Peace be unto you," and then invited them to handle his hands and his feet, that they might assure themselves that it was him, for he said, "A spirit hath not flesh and bones, as ye see me have" (Luke 24:36, 39). From this we deduce that a spirit differs in appearance from a resurrected or mortal being only in that their bodies are not physical or tangible. In all other matters they are alike.

What is of particular importance here is how a bad doctrine immediately affects everything else that it comes in contact with. In the theology of the traditional Christian world, when God lost his body so did all other eternal beings. This means that Christ had a corporeal body when he was resurrected and made such a point about walking the Emmaus road with two disciples who did not discern him as being other than mortal, appeared in the upper room and had all present place their hands in the wounds in his hands and feet and then ate before them so that they would all be witnesses of the corporeal nature of his body. When he ascended into heaven he gave them the promise that when he returned he would appear the same. All this is lost in the idea that there is no corporeality in heaven.

Our revelation tells us, "When the Savior shall appear we shall see him as he is. We shall see that he is a man like ourselves" (D&C 130:1). In his discourse on the Second Comforter, he said, "If a man love me, he will keep my words: and my Father will love him, and we will come unto him, and make our abode with him" (John 14:23). Latter-day Saints read such expressions and see them as actual and real. Joseph Smith said, "John 14:23—The appearing of the Father and the Son, in that verse, is a personal appearance; and the idea that the Father and the Son dwell in a man's heart is an old sectarian notion, and is false" (D&C 130:3).

Our understanding is based on the plainness of modern revelation. Despite the confusion that exists, many that we talk to who are not of our faith will share the same views with us because they seem so natural and right. For the most part, in doing so they have no idea that their views are in contravention to the formal tenets of the faith they espouse.

Having noted that bad doctrines infect each other, it is also interesting to note the converse. Good doctrines always have the effect of preparing the way for other good doctrines. Hence revelation comes line upon line, precept upon precept, each building on and expanding that which came before it.

Enoch's Prophecy

In a prophetic description of the events of the last days, Enoch recorded the Lord as saying, "Righteousness will I send down out of heaven; and truth will I send forth out of the earth, to bear testimony of mine Only Begotten; his resurrection from the dead; yea, and also the resurrection of all men; and righteousness and truth will I cause to sweep the earth as with a flood, to gather out mine elect from the four quarters of the earth" (Moses 7:62).

The righteousness that is to descend from heaven, as foretold to Enoch, would embrace all the revelations of the Restoration—but most particularly it applies to the appearance of the Father and the Son to Joseph Smith in the First Vision. Both the Father and the Son are resurrected beings. Then came a host of angelic ministrants such as Moroni, who led Joseph Smith to the gold plates; John the Baptist, who restored the Aaronic Priesthood; Peter, James, and John, who restored the Melchizedek Priesthood; and Adam, Raphael, Moses, Elias, Elijah, and others, who restored the various keys of the priesthood. All of these men, with the exception of the John the Revelator, who is a translated being, were resurrected beings at the time of their appearance. Their coming constitutes a perfect evidence of the reality of the resurrection. As resurrected beings, their appearance also constitutes a testimony of the reality of the resurrection.

The truth that Enoch saw coming forth from the ground is an obvious reference to the Book of Mormon, which has the same purpose, namely, to testify of Christ and his visit to the Americas as a resurrected being and of his divine Sonship. Thus it is that the story of the Restoration—centering in the First Vision and the Book of Mormon—is destined to sweep the earth as with a flood and to gather the elect back to the covenants God made anciently with their forefathers. Such a testimony is foundational to our message.

CHAPTER 12

THE CHRIST OF
THE GOSPELS

As Latter-day Saints, we are grateful beyond measure for the testimony of Christ and his earthly ministry as it has been preserved for us in the Gospels as found in the New Testament. That testimony has been confirmed to our souls by the power of the Holy Ghost. Our testimony is held in suspicion by many in the historical Christian world because of our acceptance of other books of scripture. Yet each of these books of scripture stand as independent witnesses of the truthfulness of the Bible and its testimony of Christ. Ours is a living witness. What better evidence could there possibly be that Christ lives than his appearance to the Prophet Joseph Smith? What better evidence could there be that Christ called and ordained a quorum of twelve Apostles and gave them the power and authority to act in his name than to have the three chief Apostles of that quorum appear to Joseph Smith and Oliver Cowdery and lay their hands on their heads and confer upon them the very priesthood and keys given them by Christ himself? What better evidence could you have of the ministering of angels as recorded in both the Old Testament and the New than the ministering of angels in our day? What better evidence could possibly be afforded that the meridian Twelve were granted the necessary revelation to lead and direct the kingdom of God on earth than the existence of twelve Apostles in our day doing precisely the same thing? What better evidence can you have that Christ and his disciples worked miracles than membership in a Church in which the same miracles are experienced? We have no difficulty believing the New Testament and its story of Christ and his ministry for that story is in a very real sense our story.

THE NATIVITY STORY

As Latter-day Saints we believe in the story of Christ's birth as it was recorded by Matthew and Luke. We believe him to be the actual and literal Son of God. We believe in the doctrine of the fatherhood of God. There are about 240 instances in the New Testament where the Father addresses the Son or the Son the Father. In every instance where Christ addresses the God of heaven he does so referring to him as Father. In Gethsemane Christ prayed, "Abba, Father" (Mark 14:36). "Abba" would properly be translated as "Papa" or "Daddy." The feelings that it carries with it are so tender it is difficult to utter them without it causing your lip to tremble and your eyes to fill with tears. In every instance in which the Father responds to Jesus, he uses the term Son. All of this carries a sacred feeling with it for Latter-day Saints. We cannot imagine that what we are reading is anything less than a loving father addressing his son. It is beyond our ability to construe this to mean that a spirit essence without body, parts, or passions is addressing *logos,* or some mystical representation of his own mind and will. "In the beginning," John wrote, "was the Word, and the Word was with God, and the Word was God" (John 1:1). In the Joseph Smith Translation (JST) this text reads, "In the beginning was the *gospel preached through the Son and the gospel was the word, and the word was with the Son, and the Son was with God, and the Son was of God."*

We tell the story of Christ's birth with the understanding that the shepherds who came to pay homage to him that night, though men of humble means, had been chosen in the councils of heaven to be the first earthly witnesses of his birth. We have no difficulty believing that they held the Aaronic Priesthood and thus the authority to prepare the way before him, and that the flocks they tended were the temple flocks from which would be taken those lambs which would be offered as a similitude of his atoning sacrifice. We do not believe that the wise men who came from the east were star worshipers or priests of Zoroaster but rather that they were prophets of the Lord holding the higher or Melchizedek Priesthood and that they returned to their scattered branches of Israel as special witnesses of the birth of God's Son.

The Preparatory Years

As to the youthful years of Jesus we have no part with paltry stories found in apocryphal sources that tell us of his molding birds of clay and then breathing into them the breath of life or his turning wayward playmates into statues of stone. We find no edification in stories of animals worshiping him or trees bowing to offer him their fruit. We do, however, note with keen interest that Luke's account of the twelve year old Jesus lost to Joseph and Mary for three days and found in the temple "sitting in the midst of the doctors, both hearing them, and asking them questions," is changed in the JST to read, "and they were hearing him, and asking him questions" (JST, Luke 2:46). It was not for the Son of God to be schooled in rabbinical wisdom. Again we note this addition to the third chapter of Matthew: "And it

115

came to pass that Jesus grew up with his brethren, and waxed strong, and waited upon the Lord for the time of his ministry to come. And he served under his father, and he spake not as other men, neither could he be taught; for he needed not that any man should teach him. And after many years, the hour of his ministry drew nigh" (JST, Matthew 3:24–26). This expression would not be properly understood were one to suppose that Joseph and Mary did not teach the child entrusted to them. Of course they did. It does, however, mean that his understanding was founded in the Spirit of revelation not in the learning of men. The principle is the same for all who would serve the Lord as illustrated in the instruction given to missionaries that they are to go forth to teach and not to be taught (see D&C 43:15).

He Complied with the Laws and Ordinances of the Gospel

By deliberate choice the God of heaven had his son raised in a home that was wholly observant of and obedient to the rituals of the Law of Moses. If the law was to be a schoolmaster to the house of Israel to prepare them to receive the Messiah then surely that same law constituted an able teacher for the Messiah himself. This suggests that his journey to the temple at the age of twelve was not an isolated experience but would have been followed year after year. The house of his understanding would have been built from such experiences. Before he commenced his mortal ministry he was baptized at the hands of John. This too would have accorded with the law and shown respect to the true authority by which that ordinance was preformed. Only after having been baptized himself could he rightfully command all others to be baptized in like manner. Earlier we noted the statement of Joseph Smith's that "If a man gets a fullness of the priesthood of God he has to get it in the same way that Jesus Christ obtained it, and that was by keeping all the commandments and obeying all the ordinances of the house of the Lord."[1] Our testimony is that Jesus' example in all things was most perfect.

His Ministry in Palestine

Following his baptism, Christ was, according to the traditional rendering of the text, "led up of the Spirit into the wilderness to be tempted of the devil" (Matthew 4:1). As Latter-day Saints we enjoy an improvement upon such texts. Surely the Spirit does not lead anyone into situations in which they might be tempted, let alone the Son of God. The JST tells us that Christ went into the wilderness to *"to be with God,"* which we hold to be a much better doctrine. In telling the story of his temptations the JST consistently changes the texts that have Christ being led from place to place to be tempted to having the evil one show up after the Spirit has taken Christ to these places. For instance in JST, Matthew 4:2 we read, "And when he had fasted forty days and forty nights, and *had communed with God, he was afterwards an hungered, and was left to be tempted of the devil."* We then read that it was that Spirit that took Jesus to the holy city and set him on the pinnacle of the temple and that it was the same Spirit that took him to the high mountain. These experiences would have been part of the instruction he was being given by the Father preparatory to the commencement of his ministry. We are far more comfortable with the idea that the Father was his tutor rather than the devil.

There is a good deal of confusion in the historical Christian world as to whether Christ organized a church or was embarrassed by the idea and left it to his disciples to attend to after his death. As Latter-day Saints we share no such embarrassment. We know he organized a church among the Nephites and placed the quorum of the Twelve at its head. We know that he followed the same pattern in our dispensation. In an interesting addition to the ancient text in JST, Matthew 9:18–21 we read the following discussion between Jesus and the Pharisees. "Then said the Pharisees unto him, Why will ye not receive us with our baptism, seeing we keep the whole law? But Jesus said unto them, Ye keep not the law, If ye had kept the law, ye would have received me, for I am he who gave the law. I receive not you with your baptism, because it profiteth you nothing. For when that which is new is come, the old is ready to be put away."

We would number this among the plain and precious texts that have been lost from the New Testament. From it we learn that baptism was commonly practiced in Jesus' day and that the Pharisees who were exacting in keeping the law had been baptized but that Jesus required a new baptism of his followers. That baptism identified him as the promised Messiah and symbolized their acceptance of a new order of things replacing the law of Moses. We know by way of revelation that John the Baptist was ordained by an angel of God to "overthrow the kingdom of the Jews, and to make straight the way of the Lord" (D&C 84:28). John was true to his commission in teaching Christ and administering a legal and lawful baptism.

CHRIST PRAYED TO AND TAUGHT THE DOCTRINE OF HIS FATHER

In his mortal ministry Christ prayed to his Father and taught us to do likewise. In John chapters 3 through 17 we have over 120 instances in which Christ tells us that he came to do the will of the Father and that his doctrines were the doctrines of

the Father; the JST adds a dozen more. In his great intercessory prayer recorded in John 17 he says, "And this is life eternal,
that they might know thee the only true God, and Jesus Christ,
whom thou hast sent" (John 17:3). We believe the words of John
that eternal life is to be found in our being reconciled to the Father through the Son. We believe that Christ was indeed praying
to his Father and that in death he commended his spirit into the
hand of his Father. We do not believe that we are to reject the
plain meaning of text after text with the idea that the Father and
the Son are one and the same. We do not believe that Christ was
praying to himself or that he was speaking in some figurative
sense in the hundreds of instances in which he testified of the
Father. We believe that he used the word *father* to mean just that.

GETHSEMANE

As to the account of Christ's Atonement it ought to be observed that the text in Luke that tells us that an angel came to
strengthen Christ in Gethsemane and that he sweat great drops
of blood is not found in some of the earliest manuscripts and is
thus believed by some scholars to be an embellishment by later
Christian scribes. Latter-day Saints confidently accept this text.
In a marvelous messianic prophecy, King Benjamin declared,
"And lo, he shall suffer temptations, and pain of body, hunger,
thirst, and fatigue, even more than man can suffer, except it be
unto death; for behold, blood cometh from every pore, so great
shall be his anguish for the wickedness and the abominations of
his people" (Mosiah 3:7). And again in a revelation given to Joseph Smith, we are told that the unrepentant will suffer even as
Christ suffered, "Which suffering caused myself, even God, the
greatest of all, to tremble because of pain, and to bleed at every
pore, and to suffer both body and spirit—and would that I might

119

not drink the bitter cup, and shrink" (D&C 19:18). While the historical Christian world has centered their attention on the suffering of Christ on the cross, we as Latter-day Saints turn our attention to Gethsemane. With no disrespect intended we note that he was crucified between two thieves and that as history sadly attests tens of thousand of others also died on the cross. While such a death was horrible beyond description, it was not unique to Christ.

We believe that it was in Gethsemane that

> Jesus took upon himself the sins of the world on conditions of repentance. It was there he suffered beyond human power to endure. It was there he sweat great drops of blood from every pore. It was there his anguish was so great he fain would have let the bitter cup pass. It was there he made the final choice to follow the will of the Father. It was there that an angel from heaven came to strengthen him in his greatest trial. Many have been crucified but only one, he who had God as his Father, has bowed beneath the burden of grief and sorrow that lay upon him in that awful night, that night in which he descended below all things as he prepared himself to rise above them all.[2]

Such an expression is not intended to disassociate Calvary and Christ's suffering on the cross from the Atonement. We believe that the agony of Gethsemane returned again to Christ as he hung on the cross. The agony of which we speak was in addition to or far beyond that of the cross itself. Surely the cross does not make saviors of all who shared its agonies.

Thus it is that once again we part with the historical Christian community in that we do not use the cross as a symbol of our faith.

The cross is the symbol of a dying Christ. Our faith centers in the testimony of a living Christ. The symbol of our faith must be the testimony that is evidenced in our lives and that we bear of him.

THE OPENING OF THE PRISON TO THEM THAT ARE BOUND

In a prophetic description of Christ's ministry, Isaiah said that the Savior would "proclaim liberty to the captives, and the opening of the prison to them that are bound" (Isaiah 61:1). To formally commence his ministry, Christ, in a synagogue in Nazareth, called for the scroll of Isaiah and read the text that embraces this prophecy. His announcement that this text would find its fulfillment in him was greeted by shouts of blasphemy and the attempt to hurl him from a cliff (see Luke 4:16–32). The meaning of this phrase still escapes the understanding of traditional Christianity while it finds a very direct fulfillment in his visit to the world of the spirits and his teaching the gospel, as John promised he would to them that were dead (see John 5:25–28). These verses from John's revelation in turn led the Prophet Joseph Smith and Sidney Rigdon to inquire of the Lord for understanding and then to be granted the privilege of witnessing the great revelation on the degrees of glory known to us as the Vision (D&C 76) and Christ's ministry to those in spirit prison as detailed in the vision of the redemption of the dead (D&C 138).

THE RESURRECTION

With Christians the world over, we rejoice in the New Testament account of the resurrection of Christ. We love the story all the more because of the added light and knowledge that has been given to us. In a single sentence written by the spirit of revelation we find more light and truth than in the combination of all that the finest scholars of the world have been able to write. Of the resurrected beings we are told, "Their sleeping dust was to be restored unto its perfect frame, bone to his bone, and the sinews and the flesh upon them, the spirit and the body to be united never again to be divided, that they might receive a fulness of joy" (D&C 138:17). So it is that we know that the resurrection is actual and literal. In the resurrection, a man will be a man and a woman a woman. Gender will be preserved as will be the love that exists between husband and wife and between parents and their children. The family unit can be preserved in a heaven that will be as tangible and as real as the world in which we presently live. All that is good, all that is of God that exists here will exist there in the splendor of its perfection. Everything in this world of beauty and goodness will be preserved in that world. The fruit tree, the flower garden, the songbird, and all that are like unto them will come forth in the morning of the first resurrection. As Christ charged those with whom he met in the upper room on the eve of earth's first Easter Sunday, saying, "Ye are witnesses of these things," so are we (Luke 24:48).

Notes

1. Smith, *Teachings*, 308.
2. Bruce R. McConkie, *Doctrinal New Testament Commentary*, 3 vols. (Salt Lake City: Bookcraft, 1973) 1:774–75.

CHAPTER 13

ANOTHER TESTAMENT OF CHRIST

WE have a wonderful Old Testament story where the Prophet Ezekiel is directed by the Lord to take a "stick," most probably meaning a wooden writing board, and write upon it these words: "For Judah, and for the children of Israel his companions." The Lord then told him to take another "stick" or writing board and write upon it these words, "For Joseph, the stick of Ephraim, and for all the house of Israel his companions." Ezekiel is then instructed to place these two "sticks" (or writing boards) together so that he can hold them in his hand. He is to do this while his people watch so that they will ask what is meant by his doing so. When his people ask what this little drama is intended to illustrate, he is directed to say,

> Thus saith the Lord God; Behold, I will take the children of Israel from among the heathen, whither they be gone, and will gather them on every side, and bring them into their own land:
>
> And I will make them one nation in the land upon the mountains of Israel; and one king shall be king to

them all: and they shall be no more two nations, neither shall they be divided into two kingdoms any more at all:

Neither shall they defile themselves any more with their idols, nor with their detestable things, nor with any of their transgressions: but I will save them out of all their dwelling places, wherein they have sinned, and will cleanse them: so shall they be my people, and I will be their God.

The Lord further instructs Ezekiel to tell his people that his servant "David" (meaning Christ as the son of David, who is to rule over them forever) shall be king over them and "they all shall have one shepherd," and, the Lord said, "they shall also walk in . . . my statutes, and do them." Thereafter they are to dwell in the lands that the Lord promised their fathers. "I will make a covenant of peace with them," the Lord said, and "it shall be an everlasting covenant with them: and I will place them, and multiply them, and will set my sanctuary in the midst of them for evermore." In this yet future day when Israel, now lost and scattered, have returned to the God of their fathers, the Lord said, "I will be their God, and they shall be my people. And the heathen shall know that I the Lord do sanctify Israel, when my sanctuary [meaning temple] shall be in the midst of them for evermore" (Ezekiel 37:15–28).

A Gathering to Christ and His House in the Last Days

In this interesting enactment, in which Ezekiel is directed to put the record of Judah and the record of Joseph together as one in his hand, the Lord foretells the manner in which the children of Israel who have wandered from the truth—only to find themselves in bondage, both temporally and spiritually—are to be restored to the knowledge and glory that were once theirs. From it we learn that the gathering is to take place when the Bible (or stick of Judah) and the Book of Mormon (which we know by revelation to be the stick of Joseph) are brought together as one (see D&C 27:5). Ezekiel and the prophets of the Book of Mormon place the story of the latter-day gathering in the context of Israel's return to Christ and the covenant God made with their fathers. This new covenant, which Ezekiel describes as "everlasting," is associated with the restoration of his holy sanctuary or temple among them.

Of particular interest to the story we now tell is the promise that these two independent records, both of which were written to testify of Christ, will come together as one. This, of course, accords with the divine law of witnesses, which holds that any truth that must be embraced to obtain salvation will be attested to by two or more witnesses. Thus the Book of Mormon stands as an independent witness of the truthfulness of the Bible and its testimony relative to Christ, but it also restores to us much that has been lost to the biblical record as it has been handed down to us through the ages.

THE BOOK OF MORMON AND ITS TESTIMONY OF CHRIST

The testimony of Christ as found in the Book of Mormon is so expansive that it will influence every chapter in this work. The emphasis of this chapter will be confined to the role of the Book of Mormon as a second witness of Christ and of its role in the restoration of the covenant he made with their fathers anciently. The Lord's people have always been a covenant people, and as the Book of Mormon teaches us, it is in and through that covenant that they become competent witnesses of him.

The divine commission rests with the covenant people to be the witnesses of Christ and the saving principles of his gospel. Wherever we find his people, we rightfully expect to find that testimony. Christ hinted at this when he said to the Jews of his day, "And other sheep I have, which are not of this fold: them also I must bring, and they shall hear my voice; and there shall be one fold, and one shepherd" (John 10:16). The reference to scattered sheep being brought back to the fold of the true shepherd is clearly rooted in Old Testament imagery, including the words we just quoted from Ezekiel.

In fulfillment of this prophecy, the Book of Mormon records the Savior's visit to the seed of Abraham in the New World. Christ told those who had gathered together to hear him that they were "a remnant of the house of Joseph" and that this (the American continent) had been given to them as their land of inheritance. He then added,

> And not at any time hath the Father given me commandment that I should tell it unto your brethren at Jerusalem.
>
> Neither at any time hath the Father given me commandment that I should tell unto them concerning the other tribes of the house of Israel, whom the Father hath led away out of the land.
>
> This much did the Father command me, that I should tell unto them:
>
> That other sheep I have which are not of this fold; them also I must bring, and they shall hear my voice; and there shall be one fold, and one shepherd.
>
> And now, because of stiffneckedness and unbelief they understood not my word; therefore I was commanded to say no more of the Father concerning this thing unto them.

But, verily, I say unto you that the Father hath commanded me, and I tell it unto you, that ye were separated from among them because of their iniquity; therefore it is because of their iniquity that they know not of you.

And verily, I say unto you again that the other tribes hath the Father separated from them; and it is because of their iniquity that they know not of them.

And verily I say unto you, that ye are they of whom I said: Other sheep I have which are not of this fold; them also I must bring, and they shall hear my voice; and there shall be one fold, and one shepherd.

And they understood me not, for they supposed it had been the Gentiles; for they understood not that the Gentiles should be converted through their preaching.

And they understood me not that I said they shall hear my voice; and they understood me not that the Gentiles should not at any time hear my voice—that I should not manifest myself unto them save it were by the Holy Ghost.

But behold, ye have both heard my voice, and seen me; and ye are my sheep, and ye are numbered among those whom the Father hath given me. (3 Nephi 15:12–24)

The importance of a second witness is evidenced by the great diversity of beliefs extant in the Bible-believing world. The place and purpose of baptism provides a perfect example. Among Bible believers, we find some who hold that baptism is a figurative thing representing only the need to be born again within our hearts. Others declare it to be a saving ordinance, meaning that no one can obtain salvation without having been baptized. Among those so claiming are some who perform the ordinance by sprinkling, while others claim immersion to be essential. Some baptize infants, while others hold that one must be old enough to be fully accountable for one's actions. Some claim the necessity of authority to perform this and other gospel ordinances, while others eschew the very idea of priesthood authority. It is hard to imagine how a matter of such simplicity can be surrounded by so much confusion. This illustrates why two independent witnesses are necessary.

The principle can be illustrated by making a dot on a piece of paper and then asking the question, "How many straight lines can be drawn that exactly intersect it?" If the lines could be drawn thin enough, the answer would be infinite. Suppose a second dot is made on the paper and the question is asked, "How many straight lines can be drawn that exactly intersect both dots?" The response must be that only one line can intersect both points. The necessity of having two dots to identify a sure, straight path illustrates the necessity of having two witnesses to sustain all saving truths; without them confusion reigns.

The testimony of Christ as it comes to us from the traditional Christian world is as confused as the principle of baptism. As Latter-day Saints we hold Christ to be the Son of God, while others claim him to be one and the same with the Father. We claim him to have been resurrected with a tangible or corporeal body, which he retains throughout the endless expanses of eternity. Others hold that this tangible body represented only a temporary state and that he is now without body or form of any sort. A host of other differences exist; and thus to have a sure path, a certain doctrine, one born of revelation rather than philosophical speculation, we need a second witness. As Latter-day Saints, our testimony is that God intended us to know him and his Only Begotten Son, that we might labor to become like them. That testimony finds its counterpart in the testimony of those who maintain that any meaningful understanding of God is beyond the comprehension of men and that it is intended that he remain a mystery.

While the creeds of men seek to distance them from their God, the Book of Mormon seeks to bring them together. Explaining the relationship between the Bible and the Book of Mormon, Lehi quoted these words from a prophecy that the Lord had made to Joseph of Egypt many years before:

> But a seer will I raise up out of the fruit of thy loins; and unto him will I give power to bring forth my word unto the seed of thy loins—and not to the bringing forth my word only, saith the Lord, but to the convincing them of my word, which shall have already gone forth among them.
>
> Wherefore, the fruit of thy loins shall write; and the fruit of the loins of Judah shall write; and that which shall be written by the fruit of thy loins, and also that which shall be written by the fruit of the loins of Judah, shall grow together unto the confounding of false doctrines and laying down of contentions, and establishing peace among the fruit of thy loins, and bringing them to the knowledge of their fathers in the latter days, and also to the knowledge of my covenants, saith the Lord. (2 Nephi 3:11–12)

Continual Revelation

Worlds without end, true religion will never be found seeking to seal the heavens, or to enshrine darkness over light, ignorance over intelligence, or the philosophies of men over the revelations of God. Of all our scriptural records, none can match the Book of Mormon for the eloquence with which it declares the necessity of continual revelation. Nephi stated the matter thus:

Yea, wo be unto him that hearkeneth unto the precepts of men, and denieth the power of God, and the gift of the Holy Ghost! . . .

And in fine, wo unto all those who tremble, and are angry because of the truth of God! For behold, he that is built upon the rock receiveth it with gladness; and he that is built upon a sandy foundation trembleth lest he shall fall.

Wo be unto him that shall say: We have received the word of God, and we need no more of the word of God, for we have enough!

For behold, thus saith the Lord God: I will give unto the children of men line upon line, precept upon precept, here a little and there a little; and blessed are those who hearken unto my precepts, and lend an ear unto my counsel, for they shall learn wisdom; for unto him that receiveth I will give more; and from them that shall say, We have enough, from them shall be taken away even that which they have. (2 Nephi 28:26, 28–30)

In these words Nephi teaches us that those who advocate what is called the doctrine of sufficiency, which holds that the Bible is sufficient and that no revelation beyond what is contained therein will ever be necessary, not only fail to gain all that they could have had, but they also lose the understanding of that with which they began. All who are in the Catholic, Protestant, and Evangelical worlds espouse the doctrine of sufficiency. Uniformly they declare the heavens to be sealed and revelation as it is found in the scriptures to have ceased with the death of the Apostles. The effect of such a doctrine is to close the eyes and ears of those who choose to believe it to the words of the true servants of God in our day. Not only does this place them in the unenviable position of telling the Lord that he cannot speak again and that should he do so they will not listen, but it also means, as Nephi said, that they will lose the understanding of those revelations they now have.

Those of the traditional Christian world use the same Bible we do. Yet a Latter-day Saint can pick up the Bible and teach about the premortal life, the teaching of the gospel in the world of the spirits, the place and necessity of temples in our day, prophecies relative to the coming forth of the Book of Mormon, ordinances for the dead, and countless other things that the eyes of our friends of other faiths cannot see. Theirs is a historical faith; ours is a living faith. While many of their number have a great reverence for the Bible, they have lost the key of understanding, which is the spirit of revelation. Joseph and Oliver, having complied with the ordinance of baptism and thus being entitled to the companionship of the Holy Ghost, described the difference thus: "We were filled with the Holy Ghost, and rejoiced in the God of our salvation. Our minds being now enlightened, we began to have the scriptures laid open to our understandings, and the true meaning and intention of their more mysterious passages revealed unto us in a manner which we never could attain to previously, nor ever before had thought of" (JS–H 1:73–74).

The Place of Covenants

One of the singularly significant things the Book of Mormon adds to our testimony of Christ is the place and importance of covenants in coming to an understanding of him. The Lord's people have always been a covenant people, and as it naturally follows, they have always been a temple-building people. As a people, they have known that the knowledge of Christ essential to salvation can be obtained only in and through the ordinances of salvation.

Nephi identifies this principle in his description of the return of Israel to the covenants of their fathers in the last days. "And at that day shall the remnant of our seed know that they are of the house of Israel, and that they are the covenant people of the Lord; and then shall they know and come to the knowledge of their forefathers, and also to the knowledge of the gospel of their Redeemer, which was ministered unto their fathers by him; wherefore, they shall come to the knowledge of their Redeemer and the very points of his doctrine, that they may know how to come unto him, and be saved" (1 Nephi 15:14).

Our traditional thought pattern is that only after we have learned about Christ can we enter into covenants with him. What the Book of Mormon prophets are teaching is that it is only in and through covenants that the knowledge necessary for salvation can be obtained. An understanding of what is involved is unfolded to us in a revelation given to the Prophet Joseph Smith. It reads in part: "And the Spirit giveth light to every man that cometh into the world; and the Spirit enlighteneth every man through the world, that hearkeneth to the voice of the Spirit. And every one that hearkeneth to the voice of the Spirit cometh unto God, even the Father. And the Father teacheth him of the covenant which he has renewed and confirmed upon you" (D&C 84:46–48). This is to say that the knowledge of Christ given us by the light of Christ is intended to lead us to the knowledge of the covenants of salvation, through which we obtain that knowledge necessary for salvation.

The Book of Mormon prophets consistently speak of coming to the covenant and then coming to the knowledge of Christ. This is the message of its title page, which says the Book of Mormon was written to "show unto the remnant of the House of Israel what great things the Lord hath done for their fathers;

and that they may know the covenants of the Lord, that they are not cast off forever—And also to the convincing of the Jew and Gentile that Jesus is the Christ."

Mormon, the prophet after whom the book is named, wrote thus:

> Yea, and surely shall he again bring a remnant of the seed of Joseph to the knowledge of the Lord their God.
>
> And as surely as the Lord liveth, will he gather in from the four quarters of the earth all the remnant of the seed of Jacob, who are scattered abroad upon all the face of the earth.
>
> And as he hath covenanted with all the house of Jacob, even so shall the covenant wherewith he hath covenanted with the house of Jacob be fulfilled in his own due time, unto the restoring all the house of Jacob unto the knowledge of the covenant that he hath covenanted with them.
>
> And then shall they know their Redeemer, who is Jesus Christ, the Son of God; and then shall they be gathered in from the four quarters of the earth unto their own lands, from whence they have been dispersed; yea, as the Lord liveth so shall it be. Amen. (3 Nephi 5:23–26)

All within the Church understand that you must enter into the covenant of baptism before you receive the gift of the Holy Ghost. The Holy Ghost is a revelator. Thus the great revelations you receive relative to Christ grow out of that covenant; they do not precede it. As it is with baptism, so it is with the priesthood, the temple endowment, or eternal marriage. In each instance, the greater revelation grows out of entering and keeping the covenant involved. Covenants constitute the keys that unlock understanding to us that otherwise we could not have. Thus it is that we say that the Lord's people always have been and must always be a covenant people.

In 2 Nephi 31, Nephi explains to us why Christ had to be baptized. In doing so he is describing a very different Christ than that of the traditional Christian world. He is telling us that Christ had to be baptized in order to work out his own salvation and in order to comply with the commandments of his Father in becoming a rightful heir to the companionship of the Holy Ghost (see 2 Nephi 31:7). All the blessings of heaven are conditioned on our obedience to gospel law. That law applied to Christ in precisely the same manner as it applies to us. Were this not the case, Christ's life would be of no real value to us as a pattern to follow. So it is that Joseph Smith said, "If a man gets a fullness of the priesthood of God he has to get it in the same way that Jesus Christ obtained it, and that was by keeping all the commandments and obeying all the ordinances of the house of the Lord."[1]

COVENANTS ESSENTIAL TO A COMPETENT TESTIMONY

If we take the testimony of the Book of Mormon prophets to be true—that we cannot come to a saving knowledge of Christ independent of the covenants of salvation—it must also follow that we cannot be competent witnesses of Christ independent of those covenants. Faith, repentance, baptism, and receipt of the Holy Ghost must precede our having been born again. Obedience precedes spiritual manifestations. The gifts and blessings of the Spirit follow our complying with the laws and ordinances of the gospel; they do not precede them, nor can they be had independent of them.

What we know as the Old Testament could more properly be titled the Everlasting Covenant. What we call the New Testament could more properly be titled the Restored Covenant. The Greek word that has been translated "new" in this title does not mean newly born or newly created but rather "renewed" or "restored." In both instances it is the "new and everlasting covenant" to which reference is being made. The idea being expressed by this phrase is that the covenant is "new" to our day, though "everlasting" in its nature, meaning that it is and has been the same for all people in all ages. Modern revelation refers to the Book of Mormon as "the new covenant," meaning the timeless gospel restored anew for the salvation of humankind in this the final great gospel dispensation (see D&C 84:57). So it is that we join with Malachi in bearing testimony of Christ as "the messenger of the covenant" (Malachi 3:1).

NOTE

1. Smith, *Teachings*, 308.

CHAPTER 14

THE SALVATION OF LITTLE CHILDREN

No scene in this life is more tender than that of a mother being called upon to surrender her newly born child to the arms of death. How could a loving God allow such sorrow? How can we justify the thought that there is a divine purpose in life when all that life can afford is taken from the infant child before he or she can reach out and embrace it? Surely if there is such a thing as true religion, it ought to provide a meaningful answer to such questions. Through the long night of apostate darkness, between the death of the Apostles in the Old World and the restoration of the gospel in the New, not only was the voice of heaven silenced on such matters, but parading in its place were such answers as to challenge the desire of any to believe in God or to suppose him to be anything other than heartless and cruel. What, then, is the testimony we bear?

CHRIST HAS A SPECIAL LOVE FOR LITTLE CHILDREN

Following the pattern of this work, we confine our commentary to those things that are exclusive to the revelations of the Restoration. As to the place of little children in true religion, we first note two stories, both associated with the teachings of Christ during his mortal ministry. In the first instance, parents sought to present their little children to Christ that he might bless them. His disciples rebuked them. "But Jesus said, Suffer little children, and forbid them not, to come unto me: for of such is the kingdom of heaven. And he laid his hands on them, and departed hence" (Matthew 19:14–15). In the Joseph Smith Translation the text is rendered thus: "Then were there brought unto him little children, that he should put his hands on them, and pray. And the disciples rebuked them saying, There is no need, for Jesus hath said, Such shall be saved. But Jesus said, Suffer little children to come unto me, and forbid them not, for of such is the kingdom of heaven."

We do not know the exact circumstances under which Christ taught to the Twelve the doctrine that little children would be saved, but in the previous chapter of Matthew we find Christ saying, "For the Son of Man is come to save that which was lost, and to call sinners to repentance; but these little ones have no need of repentance, and I will save them" (JST, Matthew 18:11). The testimony of the Book of Mormon is that "all little children are alive in Christ" and all are "partakers of salvation" (Moroni 8:22, 17).

The second scene finds us in the Americas, where the resurrected Lord ministered among the Nephites. Having prayed such a prayer as no mortal tongue can speak, he wept, "and he took their little children, one by one, and blessed them, and prayed unto the Father for them. And when he had done this he wept again" (3 Nephi 17:21–22).

Addressing the multitude he then said, "Behold your little ones. And . . . they saw the heavens open, and they saw angels descending out of heaven as it were in the midst of fire; and they came down and encircled those little ones about, and they were encircled about with fire; and the angels did minister unto them"

(3 Nephi 17:23–24). While we do not know who the angels were that ministered to these children, we know that angels are not faceless and that the normal practice is that angels minister to those for whom they have special interest; thus comes the inclination to suppose that the angels in this case included deceased ancestors of the children blessed.

Often Asked Questions about Little Children

Let us now ask and answer the most often asked questions about the salvation of little children.

Question: Are children tainted with original sin?

Answer: No! Original sin, as we have noted earlier, is a sad mistake that traces itself to Saint Augustine as a result of an unfortunate biblical mistranslation that has been corrected in modern editions of the Bible.

Question: Are children conceived in sin?

Answer: Adam and Eve fell that they might comply with the divine directive to multiply and replenish the earth. The command that we do likewise is part of the temple marriage ceremony and is expected to endure for time and all eternity. There is no sin in a man and his wife conceiving a child. Even at conception, however, the child becomes subject to death or the effects of the Fall. "The natural birth creates a natural man."[1] Thus children are born subject to the effects of the Fall. It is in this light that we understand Enoch's statement that "children are conceived in sin" (Moses 6:55). That is, because they have blood coursing through their veins Satan will have power to tempt them, and they will be subject to all the effects of Adam's Fall.

Question: Should little children be baptized?

Answer: Infant baptism is a denial of the grace of Christ and his atoning sacrifice. Mormon stated that "it is solemn mockery" to baptize little children, for they "are alive in Christ from the foundations of the world." Mormon's thought was that it is not the children who die without baptism who ought to be damned, but rather the person who condemned them to that fate for that reason (see Moroni 8:8–24).

Question: Are all who die as little children saved in the celestial kingdom?

Answer: "To this question the answer is a thunderous *yes* which echoes and re-echoes from one end of heaven to the other. Jesus taught it to his disciples. Mormon said it over and over again. Many of the prophets have spoken about it, and it is implicit in the whole plan of salvation. If it were not so the redemption would not be infinite in its application. And so, as we would expect, Joseph Smith's Vision of the Celestial Kingdom contains this statement: 'And I also beheld that all children who die before they arrive at the years of accountability are saved in the celestial kingdom of heaven.' (D&C 137:10)."[2]

Question: Does this apply to children of all races?

Answer: Of course it does. This is no different from asking if the Atonement applies alike to all peoples.

Question: How and why are little children saved?

Answer: Through the Atonement of Christ, all humankind are saved from the effects of Adam's fall, meaning that they overcome death. Little children are subject to death and thus are reconciled to the Father by the Son. God stated the matter thus: "Little children are redeemed from the foundation of the world through mine Only Begotten" (D&C 29:46).

Question: Will little children have eternal life?

Answer: To be immortal is to live forever; to have eternal life is to become as God is and live as he lives. Thus by its very nature, eternal life is found only in the eternal family unit. Abinadi said,

"Little children also have eternal life" (Mosiah 15:25). Joseph Smith said, "Children will be enthroned in the presence of God and the Lamb; . . . they will there enjoy the fullness of that light, glory and intelligence, which is prepared in the celestial kingdom."[3]

Joseph Fielding Smith taught the same truth:

The Lord will grant unto these children the privilege of all the sealing blessings which pertain to the exaltation. We were all mature spirits before we were born, and the bodies of little children will grow after the resurrection to the full stature of the spirit, and *all blessings will be theirs through their obedience, the same as if they had lived to maturity and received them on the earth.* The Lord is just and will not deprive any person of a blessing, simply because he dies before that blessing can be received. *It would be manifestly unfair to deprive a little child of the privilege of receiving all the blessings of exaltation in the world to come simply because it died in infancy.* . . . Children who die in childhood will not be deprived of any blessing. When they grow, after the resurrection, to the full maturity of the spirit, *they will be entitled to all the blessings which they would have been entitled to had they been privileged to tarry here and receive them.*[4]

Question: Are those who die as little children better off than those who remain in mortality?

Answer: Only if we fail to keep the commandments. Those taken as little children are excused from the tests of mortality. On the other hand, no one who has survived a difficult experience would trade it for any remuneration.

Question: Will little children who die ever be tested?

Answer: No. At death they go to paradise. No one apostatizes from paradise. In the resurrection they come forth from the grave with a celestial body. Resurrection is the inseparable union of body and spirit, so their status cannot be changed. Satan can no more deceive them or entice them to do wickedly than he can tempt God himself.

Question: What is the age of accountability?

Answer: Accountability is something that you grow up into. It does not come "full-bloom" at a given time. We expect obedient behavior out of children long before they are eight years of age. At the age of eight a child can be baptized; at the age of twelve a young man may hold the office of a deacon in the Aaronic Priesthood, but he cannot hold the office of a teacher or priest, nor can he drive a car, vote, or marry. Each will come in its own time. Our scripture states that Satan cannot tempt little children "until" they "begin" to become accountable (D&C 29:47). Becoming accountable is a process. A five-year-old has greater accountability than a three-year-old; a seven-year-old has greater accountability than a five-year-old. When a child is eight years of age, the Lord has said that they are sufficiently accountable to be baptized for the remission of sins, which assumes they can sin by that age (see D&C 18:42; 29:46–47; 68:27; 137:10).

THE TESTIMONY WE BEAR

Among all the children on the face of the earth, not a single one is an enemy to Christ or a friend to the adversary. It is true that countless numbers of their parents have yielded to the enticements of the flesh—and some even seek to crucify Christ afresh and put him to an open shame—yet even their little children can be said to be holy. "The natural man is an enemy to God, and has been from the fall of Adam, and will be, forever and ever, unless he yields to the enticings of the Holy Spirit, and putteth off the natural man and becometh a saint through the atonement of Christ the Lord, and becometh as a child, submissive, meek, humble, patient, full of love, willing to submit to all things which the Lord seeth fit to inflict upon him, even as a child doth submit to his father" (Mosiah 3:19).

Not only have we as a people been called upon to testify of Christ's love for little children and that they are redeemed in and through him, but we have been called on to testify against the wickedness of doctrines that stand in opposition to this great truth. Our testimony is that children, properly taught, are sufficiently accountable to be baptized at the age of eight and at that age to signify their willingness to take upon themselves his name. Our testimony must also embrace the plain declaration of scripture relative to those doctrines that deny the Atonement and bring heartache and sorrow to the innocent in their wake.

NOTES

1. McConkie, *New Witness for the Articles of Faith*, 282.
2. McConkie, "The Salvation of Little Children," 3–7.
3. Smith, *Teachings*, 200.
4. Smith, *Doctrines of Salvation*, 2:54.

CHAPTER 15

THE LIGHT OF CHRIST

ANOTHER of the distinctive doctrines restored to us in the revelations of the Restoration that is inseparably connected with our testimony is that of the Light of Christ. You may have supposed that this was a doctrine that we hold in common with Bible believers. It is not. The Bible is silent on the matter. Joseph Smith would have first learned this doctrine while translating the book of Moroni. Addressing the issues of the discerning of spirits, Moroni said, "For behold, the Spirit of Christ is given to every man, that he may know good from evil; wherefore, I show unto you the way to judge; for every thing which inviteth to do good, and to persuade to believe in Christ, is sent forth by the power and gift of Christ; wherefore ye may know with a perfect knowledge it is of God" (Moroni 7:16).

In a revelation given a few years later the Lord said, "That which is of God is light; and he that receiveth light, and continueth in God, receiveth more light; and that light groweth brighter and brighter until the perfect day" (D&C 50:24). In yet another revelation, in which we are told to live by every word that comes from the mouth of the Lord, we are told that "the word of the

Lord is truth, and whatsoever is truth is light, and whatsoever is light is Spirit, even the Spirit of Jesus Christ." This is the Spirit or light given to each person as he or she enters this world, "and the Spirit enlighteneth every man through the world, that hearkeneth to the voice of the Spirit. And every one that hearkeneth to the voice of the Spirit cometh unto God, even the Father. And the Father teacheth him of the covenant which he has renewed" in restoring the gospel in our day (D&C 84:45–48).

What this teaches us is that all revelation comes in the form of light, but that all light is not equally bright. Revelations pertaining to the salvation of men come from the Holy Ghost. One must prepare to receive the Holy Ghost by following the Light of Christ. The Light of Christ is the gift of God to all men, while the Holy Ghost is the gift of God to those who are born again through the waters of baptism. It was as essential for Christ to receive the companionship of the Holy Ghost as it was for him to be baptized. As Nephi said, "The voice of the Son came unto me, saying: He that is baptized in my name, to him will the Father give the Holy Ghost, *like unto me;* wherefore follow me, and do the things which ye have seen me do" (2 Nephi 31:12; emphasis added).

Membership in the Church is not a prerequisite to receiving a revelation from the Holy Ghost. Were this the case, no one could obtain the spiritual witness necessary to join the Church. In fact, such a spiritual confirmation is required of those we refer to as converts before they are baptized and before we lay hands upon their heads and give them the promise of the gift of the Holy Ghost.

We frequently speak of our right to the constant companionship of the Holy Ghost. We are generally left without any explanation as to what this means. We know that the intent is not to suggest that we stand in a constant deluge of revelation. It is the slothful and unwise servant who has to be commanded in all things. Perhaps an analogy, one taught me by my father, will help in distinguishing between having received a revelation from the Holy Ghost and our having the gift of the Holy Ghost.

Imagine yourself traveling in the dark of night through very rugged and difficult terrain, carefully seeking your way to a place of safety where you will be reunited with your family. Let us also suppose that a flash of lightning momentarily marks the path of safety before you.

The momentary flash of light pointing you in the direction of safety and shelter in our analogy represents a manifestation through the Holy Ghost. If you then follow the path it marked out, it will lead you to the waters of baptism at the hands of a legal administrator, who will say, as he confirms you a member of the Church, "receive the Holy Ghost," which means the "gift of the Holy Ghost." The light by which you now walk embraces the companionship of the Holy Ghost. It is the light of the gospel or, for some, the gospel in a new light. In either case, it enables you to see that which you could not see before.

It now becomes your privilege to walk, as it were, by the light of day. The light is constant, and in most instances the path you are called on to travel is clearly marked. In those instances in which it is not, you are entitled to the necessary vision, impression, or prodding necessary to assure your arrival at the place of safety.

To enjoy the "constant companionship of the Holy Ghost" means, for instance, that as you fill your assignments as a teacher in the Church, if you are prepared properly, you will be taught things from on high as you teach others. Such an experience will require more of you than the kind of presentation in which you simply repeat or rearrange the thoughts of others. The fact that every member of the Church is given the gift of the Holy Ghost is evidence that the Lord wants to reveal things to you and through you.

Possession of the Light of Christ does not require faith in God or the testimony that Jesus is the Christ. Its purpose, however, is to lead all of God's children to that end. Revelations from the Holy Ghost are of a higher order, or reach beyond the light and knowledge that is had by the generality of humankind. Light and knowledge that come from the Light of Christ are generally understood and accepted by good people everywhere. Revelations that come from the Holy Ghost are a different matter. While those revelations that come from the Light of Christ tend to unite us with the world, revelations that come from the Holy Ghost—that is, principles appended to eternal life—generally alienate us from the world.

Because they are born with the Light of Christ, all humankind are capable of discerning between good and evil and between that behavior that is proper and that which is not. Thus every soul who so much as draws a breath in this life will be held strictly to account for all their actions by a wise and just God for the manner in which they exercised their agency and what they did with the opportunities that were theirs. No one has the "right," for instance, to reject the testimony that Jesus is the Christ. Everyone can do so—that is part of agency—but they do not have the "right" to do so, only the "capacity." This is simply to say that we all have the ability to do things that are wrong, but we certainly do not have the "right" to do evil things.

Most truths known to most people have come to them by the Light of Christ. Such truths are easily identified. They lead to good; they edify and refine the soul; they purify the heart. They are found in the instinct of a mother to love and nurture her child and in the desire of a father to protect and provide for those he loves; indeed, they are the very essence of love itself. The Light of Christ is found in the encouragement that friends give one another and the comfort given those who have cause to mourn; it sparks the impulse in the hearts of all who follow its promptings to aid and lift the downtrodden. Such feelings and understandings are manifestations of the light of heaven. Truth is all this, and ten thousand times ten thousand things more, but in it all, truth or light naturally finds itself on the side of that which is right and good.

In a revelation given May 6, 1833, Christ said, "I am the true light that lighteth every man that cometh into the world" (D&C 93:2). He then went on to explain that the agency and the condemnation of man were intertwined "because that which was from the beginning is plainly manifest unto them, and they receive not the light. And every man whose spirit receiveth not the light is under condemnation" (D&C 93:31–32). What this tells us is that we all knew Christ and his gospel before we were born and before the veil of birth was drawn over our minds. Nevertheless, we are expected to be responsive to knowledge or testimony planted in our hearts; and if we are, it will lead us back to the testimony of Christ that was ours in the premortal world. If we exercise our agency so as to reject this light, it will be to our condemnation.

Christ Gives Light to All Things

Our testimony is that Joseph Smith is the great revelator of Christ for our dispensation. The evidence, of course, is in the doctrines that he revealed to us about Christ. None of those revelations is more breathtaking or expansive than the revelation he denominated the "olive leaf." Testifying that Jesus Christ is the Son of God, it says of him:

He that ascended up on high, as also he descended below
all things, in that he comprehended all things, that he
might be in all and through all things, the light of truth;

Which truth shineth. This is the light of Christ. As also he is in the sun, and the light of the sun, and the power thereof by which it was made.

As also he is in the moon, and is the light of the moon, and the power thereof by which it was made;

As also the light of the stars, and the power thereof by which they were made;

And the earth also, and the power thereof, even the earth upon which you stand.

And the light which shineth, which giveth you light, is through him who enlighteneth your eyes, which is the same light that quickeneth your understandings; . . .

The light which is in all things, which giveth life to all things, which is the law by which all things are governed, even the power of God who sitteth upon his throne, who is in the bosom of eternity, who is in the midst of all things. (D&C 88:6–11, 13)

Where else are we told that Christ is the light of the sun, the moon, and the stars? Where else do we read that there are no laws save he gave them? Where else are told that there is no power save it is his? Where else are told that there is no knowledge or intelligence save it comes from him? Where else are we told that there is no power for good save it comes of him? How puny the views of men who would have us believe that he obtained his exalted status by mastery of laws, when the testimony of holy writ is that he is the source and author of them all! How lame the notion that he is endlessly learning when the words of revelation assure us that he is the source of all knowledge, all wisdom, all understanding, that he is above all, and in all, and through all! Indeed, all things testify of him—for without him they are not.

We do not even begin to comprehend the length or breadth, the majesty or greatness of his power. Nevertheless, this we do know:

His light fills the immensity of space—it is in greater or lesser measure everywhere present.

Light is the source of his power and the law by which all things are governed.

His light is the power that gives life to all things.

His light enlightens the mind and quickens the understanding of every person born into this world.

The Light of Christ strives with men (the Holy Ghost testifies but does not strive) unless and until they rebel against light and truth, at which time it ceases to strive and withdraws from them.

Those who follow that light will receive more light, and the light will grow brighter and brighter until the perfect day.

And again, as we reach out to embrace the expanses of eternity and the God who rules over them all, we read these words:

All kingdoms have a law given;

And there are many kingdoms; for there is no space in the which there is no kingdom; and there is no kingdom in which there is no space, either a greater or a lesser kingdom.

And unto every kingdom is given a law; and unto every law there are certain bounds also and conditions.

All beings who abide not in those conditions are not justified.

For intelligence cleaveth unto intelligence; wisdom receiveth wisdom; truth embraceth truth; virtue loveth virtue; light cleaveth unto light; mercy hath compassion on mercy and claimeth her own; justice continueth its course and claimeth its own; judgment goeth before the face of him who sitteth upon the throne and governeth and executeth all things.

He comprehendeth all things, and all things are before him, and all things are round about him; and he is above all things, and in all things, and is through all things, and is round about all things; and all things are by him, and of him, even God, forever and ever.

And again, verily I say unto you, he hath given a law unto all things. (D&C 88:36–42)

The God of whom we bear witness rules all things throughout the endless expanses of eternity. There is no place in the eternities where he is without authority. There is no border that one can cross to escape his justice or hide from his wrath. He stands supreme. There is no space that is not governed by his law. The truth is not simply that God knows all things but that he constitutes the source of their existence. All things are an expression of the existence of God. Every truth, every law, every form of existence—all evidence the hand of God. He created them all; there is nothing relative to them that he does not know. Thus he is above all things, he is the source of life to all things, and he governs all things. Again, to suppose that there is a place or that there is knowledge that is presently beyond God is to suppose that in some place or in some matter God is other than, indeed less than, God. We have the testimony of God himself that this is not the case. Again, such is our testimony of Christ.

CHAPTER 16

IN HIS HOLY NAME

BEARING his testimony of Christ to the Saints in Ephesus, the Apostle Paul assured them that there is but "one Lord, one faith, one baptism" (Ephesians 4:5). There is but one path that leads back to the presence of the Father. That path is marked by Christ; and from the time Adam and Eve left Eden every revelation for the salvation of men has come from him, for he alone is the source of our salvation. Teaching this principle, Elder Bruce R. McConkie said: "All things center in Christ. He is the God of Israel, the God of the Old Testament, the Advocate, Mediator, and Intercessor. Since the fall of Adam, all of the dealings of Deity with man have been through the Son. On occasions, however, in accordance with the principle of divine investiture of authority, the Son has and does speak in the first person as though he were the Father, because the Father has put his name on the Son."[1]

In those recorded instances in which the Father has actually spoken, it has been for the purpose of introducing his Son or testifying of his divine Sonship. Thus John in his gospel declared, "And no man hath seen God at any time, except he hath borne record of the Son; for except it is through him no man can be saved" (JST, John 1:19). The principle is illustrated perfectly in the First Vision, when both the Father and the Son appeared to Joseph Smith to introduce a new gospel dispensation. The Father addressed the youthful Joseph saying, "*This is My Beloved Son. Hear Him!*" (JS–H 1:17). It was Christ that then answered Joseph's question and instructed him.

This is an internal evidence of the truthfulness of Joseph's testimony. Had Joseph come out of the grove saying that the Father and the Son appeared to him and that the Father answered his question relative to which church he should join, we would know the story to be false. The answer of necessity must have come through the Son, for the Son has been chosen by the Father to be the source of all revelations for the salvation of men in this world. This is not something that one could reasonably have expected a fourteen-year-old boy to have known.

An uncle of mine once told me that he had been asked to speak in Church on the principle of revelation. He asked if I had any suggestions. He then noted that his bishop had told him to be sure to keep his talk Christ centered. My response was that all revelations come through Christ, so of necessity they are "Christ centered." We then reviewed the principle of divine investiture of authority. No true revelation could ever deny that Jesus was the Christ, for all the revelations of heaven come through him. It is equally true that no one could have the Spirit of Christ and at the same time deny the spirit of revelation. Again, as the Revelator declared, "the testimony of Jesus is the spirit of prophecy" (Revelation 19:10).

CHANNELS

It is fundamental to the understanding of every Latter-day Saint that the God of heaven has ordained a channel through which the doctrines of salvation are to come. If individuals are to act in the name of Christ, they must be able to show that Christ placed his name upon them. This cannot be done simply by professing belief in the Bible, for the Bible tells us that "the devils also believe, and tremble" (James 2:19). The authority to act in the name of Christ is known to us as the priesthood. The concept of priesthood is simply an extension of the doctrine of divine investiture of authority. To act in the name of Christ is a very solemn and sacred responsibility. "Let all men beware how they take my name in their lips," the Lord said. "For behold, verily I say, that many there be who are under this condemnation, who use the name of the Lord, and use it in vain, having not authority" (D&C 63:61–62).

We do not simply choose to go out and declare Christ, nor do we have any right to claim the commission given by him to others thousands of years ago. President Joseph F. Smith's vision of the redemption of the dead provides a classic illustration of this principle. When Christ visited the world of the spirits, a vast multitude who had been faithful to his name in mortality was gathered together in one place. Yet none of these, including Adam, Noah, Abraham, Isaac, Jacob, Moses, Isaiah, Ezekiel, Daniel, Malachi, and the Nephite prophets—all of whom had worn out their mortal lives testifying of him—had assumed for a moment that it was their right to go forth and preach the gospel to those who had not heard it in this life, until they were commissioned to do so. Thus President Smith tells us that Christ "organized his forces and appointed messengers, clothed with power and authority, and commissioned them to go forth and carry the light of the gospel to them that were in darkness," which they then did (D&C 138:30).

"We believe," and it is an article of faith among us, "that a man must be called of God, by prophecy, and by the laying on of hands by those who are in authority, to preach the Gospel and administer in the ordinances thereof" (Articles of Faith 1:5). We are not self-called or self-ordained, nor is the message of our making. In a revelation known as "the law," meaning the law of the Church, the Lord said: "Again I say unto you, that it shall not be given to any one to go forth to preach my gospel, or to build up my church, except he be ordained by some one who has authority, and it is known to the church that he has authority and has been regularly ordained by the heads of the church" (D&C 42:11).

The Lord's house is a house of order, which it could hardly be if everyone who chose to represent him was free to do so, and it was left to each of us to determine our own plan of salvation. The Lord's house could hardly be considered a house of order if God himself kept appointing messengers that stood in violation of the principles he had established to govern the ministering of his gospel. Since God's house is a house of order, it will not be governed by laws of someone else's making, it will not honor offerings made to other gods, nor will ordinances performed without his permission or authority be acceptable to him (see D&C 132:7–13).

THE NAME OF THE CHURCH

As a people, both individually and collectively, we take upon ourselves the name of Christ. The name of the Church, one granted by revelation, is "The Church of Jesus Christ of Latter-day Saints" (see D&C 115:5). It bears his name because it is his Church. "How be it my church save it be called in my name?" (3 Nephi 27:8). Teaching this principle to the Nephite disciples, Christ said,

> For if a church be called in Moses' name then it be Moses' church; or if it be called in the name of a man then it be the church of a man; but if it be called in my name then it

is my church, if it so be that they are built upon my gospel. Verily I say unto you, that ye are built upon my gospel; therefore ye shall call whatsoever things ye do call, in my name; therefore if ye call upon the Father, for the church, if it be in my name the Father will hear you; and if it so be that the church is built upon my gospel then will the Father show forth his own works in it. (3 Nephi 27:8–10)

Thus all that is done within the Church is done in the name of Christ. "And again, I say unto you, all things must be done in the name of Christ, whatsoever you do in the Spirit; and ye must give thanks unto God in the Spirit for whatsoever blessing ye are blessed with" (D&C 46:31–32).

We obtain membership in the Church by being baptized in the name of Christ. Instructing the newly called Apostles among the Nephites relative to this ordinance, Christ said: "Behold, ye shall go down and stand in the water, and in my name shall ye baptize them. And now behold, these are the words which ye shall say, calling them by name, saying: Having authority given me of Jesus Christ, I baptize you in the name of the Father, and of the Son, and of the Holy Ghost. Amen. And then shall ye immerse them in the water, and come forth again out of the water" (3 Nephi 11:23–26). Thus by covenant we show our willingness to take his name upon us.

SPECIAL WITNESSES OF HIS NAME

The revelation given to instruct the newly called Twelve in our day states that they are to be "special witnesses of the name of Christ in all the world" (D&C 107:23). It is important for us to note that they were not simply called to be "special witnesses of Christ," but rather special witnesses of his "name." Name means authority. For instance, speaking to Abraham the Lord said, "I will lead thee by my hand, and I will take thee, to put upon thee my name, even the Priesthood of thy father, and my power shall be over thee" (Abraham 1:18). When in the performance of a priesthood ordinance we say, "In the name of Jesus Christ," it is the same as saying, "In the authority of Jesus Christ." Thus the Apostles do not simply go throughout the world testifying of Christ, but rather, they also have the responsibility to set the Church in order. When they attend a stake conference they will spend a considerable amount of time with the leadership of the stake, training and instructing them. They will make whatever changes are necessary; and then, in what could be likened to the frosting on the cake, they meet in a general session of the conference to teach and testify to the Saints.

The world is full of people who serve the Lord on their own terms and profess to testify of him. They do not, however, testify of his "name," meaning they refuse to reverence and respect his priesthood. These people argue against the necessity of the priesthood and its ordinances. They do not understand the statement of the Savior to the meridian Twelve when he said, "Ye have not chosen me, but I have chosen you, and ordained you, that ye should go and bring forth fruit, and that your fruit should remain: that whatsoever ye shall ask of the Father in my name, he may give it you" (John 15:16). Indeed, these people deny a place to the Quorum of the Twelve in their churches.

In yet another revelation given to the Twelve to explain their duties, the Lord said, "Whosoever receiveth my word receiveth me, and whosoever receiveth me, receiveth those, the First Presidency, whom I have sent, whom I have made counselors for my name's sake unto you. . . . For unto you, the Twelve, and those, the First Presidency, who are appointed with you to be your counselors and your leaders, is the power of this priesthood given, for the last days and for the last time, in the which is the dispensation of the fulness of times" (D&C 112:20, 30).

Thus it is that the Melchizedek Priesthood comes with an oath and covenant. Those holding the priesthood enter into a covenant to sustain and respect those who preside over them in the priesthood and to do their duty to assure that the Lord's house will be a house of order. In turn, the Lord swears with an oath that he will reward them with the fulness of his kingdom. Our revelation states the matter thus: "All they who receive this priesthood receive me, saith the Lord; for he that receiveth my servants receiveth me; and he that receiveth me receiveth my Father; and he that receiveth my Father receiveth my Father's kingdom; therefore all that my Father hath shall be given unto him. And this is according to the oath and covenant which belongeth to the priesthood" (D&C 84:35–39).

CHRIST AND THE PRIESTHOOD

The word *disciple* grows out of the word *discipline*; its intent is to give description to a disciplined follower. The words *ordinance* and *ordain* grow out of the world *order* and are intended to ensure order in the house of the Lord. Surely, there can be no kingdom of God unless there is some system of laws and government, for without them no kingdom can exist. As Latter-day Saints, our testimony of Christ embraces the necessity of his placing his name upon us and of our honoring and respecting his priesthood, which is the authority to act in his name. One of our great revelations on the priesthood states that "this greater priesthood [meaning the Melchizedek Priesthood] administereth the gospel" (D&C 84:19). That means the teaching of the gospel and the administering of the ordinances of salvation must take place under the direction of those the Lord has called and chosen, for only in such a system could his gospel remain his gospel.

LET EVERY MAN BEWARE

The devil does not always come in the form of a tyrant or bully; more often he delights in our "seduction" or very gentle enticement to that which is inappropriate, immodest, unclean, or untrue. "Wherefore," the Lord said, "let every man beware lest he do that which is not in truth and righteousness before me" (D&C 50:9). And so we note how common it is for us as a people to be criticized for following blindly, for submissively obeying, and for sustaining those we believe to have been called of God to lead us. It is common for those who have left the faith to clothe themselves in the pride of their newfound independence of thought and ability to see what the mindless mass of Latter-day Saints cannot see. In their individuality, they become somewhat reminiscent of our high school classmates, who all dressed alike to show that they were different.

All things have their time and place. There is a time for unity and a time for appropriate individuality. Latter-day Saints enjoy a collective power, unknown to any other organization on earth, to aid and help others—while at the same time we have an individual confidence and power that also remains unmatched because our testimonies are very much a personal thing. To the dismay of our critics, our theology prepares us to do both very effectively. The priesthood provides an excellent illustration of the point. Only in The Church of Jesus Christ of Latter-day Saints are all worthy men given the power and authority to act in the name of God. For these men to receive such a trust, they must learn how to march together as well as how to act with strength and dignity alone. To value the one function over the other or to isolate the one from the other is to corrupt both the purpose and the power of the priesthood.

In the gospel of Jesus Christ, one does not expect to find salvation separately or singly. We are a covenant people, and as such we have covenanted to sustain and support one another. Your covenants are both personal and collective; so is your strength. As there is a power that husband and wife share in the unity of their love that neither can have separately and singly, so it is with our faith. Those who revile our unified strength are much akin to those who have not experienced the strength that comes from a good marriage, a strong family, and a church in which all are known as brother and sister. The new and everlasting covenant embraces and requires both.

Taking Upon Us His Name

Either individually or collectively, we as Latter-day Saints harbor no illusions that we can save ourselves. Christ is our Savior. Salvation is in him and no other. In the hope of salvation, we take upon ourselves his name and we seek to become one in him. We honor those he has sent in his name and reverence their voice as his voice. We seek to so live that when called upon to act in his behalf we will have the faith and strength to do so. We believe this to be the right and privilege of every member of his Church. On this matter we as a Church stand alone, while in testimony we stand together.

Note

1. McConkie, *Doctrinal New Testament Commentary,* 1:77.

CHAPTER 17

HOW CHRIST GAINED HIS TESTIMONY

LET us now raise the question as to how Christ obtained his testimony. As the Son of God was he entitled at birth to a full and complete knowledge of all the principles of salvation? In his case was the veil not drawn or was it in place only for a brief period, like a morning mist that quietly disappears with the rising of the sun? Just what was required of him to obtain a comprehensive knowledge of scripture and to become a master teacher? As to faith in God and his purposes, was it naturally his or did he have to labor to obtain it as the great prophets had done before him? Was it required of him to learn line upon line, precept upon precept, here a little and there a little, as you and I do, or were wisdom and knowledge his at birth, like the color of his eyes and hair?

The answers we give to such questions directly affects the nature of the testimony we bear of him and the way we seek to emulate him. The Bible is virtually silent on such matters, but like so many other things that are foundational to our testimony, the revelations of the Restoration speak directly to the issue. This directness suggests that these answers contain principles that are important for us to understand if the testimony we bear is to be what it ought to be.

THE TESTIMONY OF JOHN THE BAPTIST

Virtually every revelation in the Doctrine and Covenants comes in response to a question addressed to the heavens by the Prophet Joseph Smith. Many of these questions were in conjunction with his labor on the Inspired Version of the Bible or, as we now call it, the Joseph Smith Translation. Others dealt with administrative matters necessary to assure that the Lord's house would continue to be a house of order. What appears to be an exception to the "ask God" pattern established by most of the revelations is what we know today as Doctrine and Covenants 93. We have no knowledge of any particular circumstances that called it forth. This revelation, which was given May 6, 1833, is also of special interest in that it is in part a restoration of a record or gospel written by John the Baptist and hidden up to come forth in some future day. Its purpose, in harmony with all that John did, was to bear testimony of Christ. Reversing the order of their mortal ministries, this record begins with the testimony of Christ relative to his own divine Sonship. Christ does so in these words:

Verily, thus saith the Lord: It shall come to pass that every soul who forsaketh his sins and cometh unto me, and calleth on my name, and obeyeth my voice, and keepeth my commandments, shall see my face and know that I am;

And that I am the true light that lighteth every man that cometh into the world;

And that I am in the Father, and the Father in me, and the Father and I are one—

The Father because he gave me of his fulness, and the Son because I was in the world and made flesh my tabernacle, and dwelt among the sons of men.

I was in the world and received of my Father, and the works of him were plainly manifest.

And John saw and bore record of the fulness of my glory, and the fulness of John's record is hereafter to be revealed. (D&C 93:1–6)

The promise here given is that Christ will manifest himself in the flesh to those who live worthy of the experience. The principle, very much a part of our testimony, cuts through the most arduously held principles of the sectarian world. Not only is it saying that revelation is to continue and that there are yet records to be added to our canon of scripture, but it teaches that such revelation can and will include the personal appearance of our Lord and Savior to his worthy disciples.

In the record kept by the Baptist, he tells of a vision in which he was shown the ministry of Christ in the premortal world. He would have learned, as did Father Abraham in a similar vision, that Christ was the most intelligent of all the heavenly hosts. Indeed, he was like unto God the Father in intelligence and glory, knowing all truth. "The great Jehovah," Joseph Smith said,

contemplated the whole of the events connected with the earth, pertaining to the plan of salvation, before it rolled into existence, or ever 'the morning stars sang together' for joy; the past, the present, and the future were and are, with Him, one eternal 'now'; He knew of the fall of Adam, the iniquities of the antediluvians, of the depth of iniquity that would be connected with the human family, their weakness and strength, their power and glory, apostasies, their crimes, their righteousness and iniquity; He comprehended the fall of man, and his redemption; He knew the plan of salvation and pointed it out; He was acquainted with the situation of all nations and with their destiny; He ordered all things according to the council of His own will; He knows the situation of both the living and the dead, and has made ample provision for their redemption, according to their several circumstances, and the laws of the kingdom of God, whether in this world, or in the world to come.[1]

Such things and more will yet be revealed to us in the record kept by John. "I saw his glory," John testified, "that he was in the beginning, before the world was; therefore, in the beginning the Word was, for he was the Word, even the messenger of salvation—the light and the Redeemer of the world; the Spirit of truth, who came into the world, because the world was made by him, and in him was the life of men and the light of men" (D&C 93:7–9).

Thus ascribing the light and life enjoyed by all men to Christ, John continued,

And I, John, bear record that I beheld his glory, as the glory of the Only Begotten of the Father, full of grace and truth, even the Spirit of truth, which came and dwelt in the flesh, and dwelt among us. And I, John, saw that he received not of the fulness at the first, but received grace for grace; and he received not of the fulness at first, but continued from grace to grace, until he received a fulness; and thus he was called the Son of God, because he received not of the fulness at the first" (D&C 93:11–14).

FROM GRACE TO GRACE

Among the great principles being revealed to us in this extract from the writings of John is that Christ, despite the majesty and glory that was his before he was born of Mary, came to earth a helpless, infant child and that he had to grow in knowledge, wisdom, and grace as all men. Be assured that the text does not suggest that he grew from gracelessness to grace, or from a man of sin to one of goodness, but rather that he grew from one grace to a greater grace.

Let us illustrate with practical questions. Is it, for instance reasonable to suppose that Christ got more out of his second reading of the Old Testament text than he did the first? Is it reasonable to suppose that he did not catch the length and breadth of Isaiah in the first reading? Is it possible that he had greater understanding at the age of fourteen than he did at the age of twelve? Is it possible that he, too, had to grow up into the Holy Ghost and a knowledge of the spirit of revelation, as all good men and women must do? Is it possible that he could continuously give better answers to questions with the passing of years as he prepared for his ministry—not that he was in error in the first instance, but that he could expand and improve in the second? Is it possible that as he was stronger at the age of eighteen than he was at fourteen, he was wiser and kinder also? Is it possible that he learned to teach by teaching and that he improved with experience? Is it possible that he exercised a particle of faith in his youth and that it grew with each passing day? Is it possible that the first miracle that he performed in his mortal ministry was not the turning of water to wine at the marriage feast in Cana—but that the reason his mother came to him for help on that occasion, with full confidence that he could do something miraculous, was that she had witnessed other such things?

CHRIST OUR EXEMPLAR

Just as we are to be good examples to one another, so it was intended that Christ be our perfect example in all things. This was true in the first estate, and it was the case with his mortal ministry. His example would be of little value if he was not faced with the same kind of challenges that we are. We know that it was required of him to "go forth, suffering pains and afflictions and temptations of every kind; and this that the word might be fulfilled which saith he will take upon him the pains and the sicknesses of his people. And he will take upon him death, that he may loose the bands of death which bind his people; and he will take upon him their infirmities, that his bowels may be filled with mercy, according to the flesh, that he may know according to the flesh how to succor his people according to their infirmities" (Alma 7:11–12).

We also know that this principle must be balanced with the reality that Christ avoided much by way of suffering, just as we can, by his obedience to the laws and ordinances of the gospel. He did not have to walk in darkness, having chosen to walk in the light. We can have every confidence that Christ utilized his agency wisely, making the best of choices when those choices were available for him to make. We can also have every confidence that the tests of mortality to which he was subject involved accepting that over which he had no control, which is often the case with each of us. We all must learn to change that which we ought to change and accept that which we cannot. Christ would not have been excused such experiences.

Of course, we cannot describe Christ's experiences in such a way that they represent the perfect reflection of every soul who ever lived, but we can have the faith that the divine plan afforded him a perfect understanding of suffering, the experience of having the light withdrawn and facing the darkness of hell, and conversely his being endowed with knowledge and power from on high. Now I am perfectly aware that it can be said that he was never an old man and thus knows little of the difficulties of old age, that since he was not a woman he cannot fully understand the difficulties particular to the feminine gender, and so forth. I think we would be wise to set all such objections aside and simply accept the assurance of heaven that in life and in his Atonement he "descended below all things" (D&C 88:6) and that his life's experience prepared him to succor all the children of God with full and complete and perfect understanding and empathy.

We certainly make no pretense to having all the answers to the manner in which Christ gained his testimony, but this we know with perfect confidence: it was granted to him line upon line according to the same principles as our testimonies will be granted to us.

Because we have been told that our prophet, the man who stands at the head of the Church and kingdom of God, will not be allowed to lead the Church astray, are we to conclude that he cannot during that period of service improve his views or his understanding of gospel principles? To advance from one grace to another hardly suggests that because one can improve one was in error. Rather it suggests that he took a correct understanding and made it more correct, he took what was good and made it even better. We have all witnessed the marvelous growth that comes to missionaries during the course of their service. Would we not want to accord the same privilege of growth to the newly called bishop, stake president, or general authority? At what point do we want to say, "They have enough, they must continue now without change or improvement"? Rather, each stage and age in life bring with it lessons of its own, lessons that build on and grow out of all that we have known and experienced previously.

Thus our whole experience in life was intended to be a quiet and unobtrusive movement forward. Knowledge, testimony, and wisdom are all things we grow up into rather than obtain at a given point. No one would say I received my education on a given day. Education is an ongoing thing. We might say that we completed a given course or part of our education at a given time or place, but the process goes on. It goes on, or it shrivels up and dies.

So it is in the realm of spiritual things. Spiritual knowledge is a living thing, and as such it must continue to grow and change. If we are to follow the path that Christ followed, we must continually seek to advance from one grace to a greater grace.

This concept captures the whole system and plan of salvation. It is an emphatic rejection of the notion that one has a special and particular experience in which they are saved. Salvation is not found in a particular moment or experience; it is found in completing the course and enduring to the end. Because of the importance of this being clearly understood, the Lord could not wait for the time when the fulness of John's record would come forth or even for the time when Joseph Smith would ask a pertinent question about this principle. Rather, the Lord chose to restore this understanding to us as a people even in the infancy of the newly restored Church.

John Seals His Testimony

Having testified that Christ advanced from grace to grace, John then said, "And I, John, bear record, and lo, the heavens were opened, and the Holy Ghost descended upon him in the form of a dove, and sat upon him, and there came a voice out of heaven saying: This is my beloved Son. And I, John, bear record that he received a fulness of the glory of the Father; and he received all power, both in heaven and on earth, and the glory of the

Father was with him, for he dwelt in him" (D&C 93:15–17). We are then assured that if we are faithful, the day will come when we will receive the fulness of the record of John (see D&C 93:18).

To assure that we have understood, the message the Lord next said, "I give unto you these sayings that you may understand and know how to worship, and know what you worship, that you may come unto the Father in my name, and in due time receive of his fulness" (D&C 93:19). As a result of this revelation, we are to have a clear understanding of "how" we are to worship and "what" we are to worship. The "how" of worship is found in advancing from grace to grace. This is to say, it is found in the daily living of the gospel. It is found in the countless things we do in the name of Christ. It is found in learning from each of life's experiences as they come to us and in constantly pressing forward. It is found in pursuing a course that is straight and true. It is found in constant effort to live as Christ lived and to do as he did.

"What" we worship is the Father. Like Christ, we seek in all things to do his will. "For if you keep my commandments," the Lord said, "you shall receive of his fulness, and be glorified in me as I am in the Father; therefore, I say unto you, you shall receive grace for grace. . . . And no man receiveth a fulness unless he keepeth his commandments. He that keepeth his commandments receiveth truth and light, until he is glorified in truth and knoweth all things" (D&C 93:20, 27–28).

We Must All Advance from Grace to Grace

The principles taught in this revelation stand at the very heart of the plan by which salvation is to be obtained. If we are to be saved we must follow Christ. We must do the kind of things he did. That is, we must learn to think as he thought, believe as he believed, and act as he acted. We must become one with him in thought and action. This makes our faith a living faith, because we are constantly called on to live it. Our faith and testimony are measured in the way we live, in the things we do. It is one thing to accept Christ; it is quite another to become like him.

It will be remembered that in his great intercessory prayer offered at the Last Supper, Christ said, "This is life eternal, that they [his disciples] might know thee the only true God, and Jesus Christ, whom thou hast sent" (John 17:3). Though the term is used with various shades of meaning, "to know God" in the purest scriptural sense is to have an intimate or covenant relationship with him. The Old Testament references to knowing God and to a man knowing his wife, meaning conceiving a child with her, both use the same Hebrew word (*yada*). As a man was to leave father and mother and cleave unto his wife and thus become one flesh with her, so he was to leave the things of the world and cleave unto his God and become one with him. As faithfulness in marriage was essential to the nurturing of love, so faithfulness in keeping gospel covenants was understood to be necessary in obtaining a knowledge of God. As love of spouse was strengthened in sacrifice and devotion, so the knowledge of God was obtained in living those covenants with exactness and honor. Thus, a frequent characteristic of Hebrew prophecy was to describe apostasy through the metaphor of adultery, and Israel's covenant with God as a marriage (see Jeremiah 2:20–37; Ezekiel 16; Hosea 1–3).

Similarly, we read in the New Testament that Joseph did not know Mary until after the birth of Christ (see Matthew 1:25); and as we just noted that it is life eternal to know God and Jesus Christ his Son. Both passages use the same Greek word (*ginosko*). The *Dictionary of the New Testament* defines knowledge in this manner:

Knowledge was not reducible to an act of the intellect that apprehended an object. The word preserves an experiential dimension that is characteristic of it: to observe, to experience, to know, to discern, to appraise, to *establish an intimate relationship between two persons, whence to choose, to elect, to enter a sexual union, finally, to recognize.* In conformity with this notion of truth, to know was to encounter someone; not to know was to thrust him aside from oneself. Knowledge of God was possible because this meant a 're-cognition' of the one who, through his creation, was already there. To know was to be disposed to obey.[2]

Again we see that fidelity was to love as righteousness was to the knowledge of God. Thus Peter lists such things as virtue, kindness, charity, and patience as requisites to knowing the Father and the Son. Independent of such attributes of godliness, all knowledge of God, he held, was "barren [or] unfruitful" (see 2 Peter 1:5–8). Texts in both the Old and the New Testament espouse the idea that one could not truly know God without that knowledge manifesting itself in the way one lived (see Deuteronomy 13:2–3; Jeremiah 22:15–16; Hosea 4:1–2; John 7:16–17).

In Greek thought, by contrast, knowledge came through the senses and consisted of that which could be verified by observation. To the Greek, knowledge was the intellectual comprehension of the realities of the world. This was the knowledge of which Paul was so critical in his epistle to the Corinthians, the knowledge of which he said "the world by wisdom knew not God" (1 Corinthians 1:21).

"The Greek thinkers supposed that they could grasp the nature of reality by applying rational processes to evaluate the data they gained by observing the universe. Paul says that the shape of reality can be known only through revelation, for God's Spirit must communicate the things known only to God. Some information about reality is simply not available to humanity through the senses, for 'No eye has seen, no ear has heard, no mind has conceived what God has prepared for those who love him.' [1 Corinthians 2:9.]"[3]

Such was the knowledge of which Christ spoke, a knowledge which he said "the world cannot receive" (John 14:17), a knowledge obtained only through obedience (see John 7:17).

This idea of sacred knowledge being obtainable only in the living of sacred covenants finds eloquent expression in the revelations of the Restoration. It was in the restoration of the Melchizedek Priesthood that we obtained "the key of the knowledge of God" (D&C 84:19), and it is a revelation concerning the priesthood in which we are told that the attributes of godliness are requisite for obtaining that knowledge (see D&C 107:30–31). Further, we are told that all such knowledge must come by revelation (see D&C 121:26), and that its nature is such that it cannot be understood by the "carnal mind" (Alma 36:4; D&C 67:12); instead, it must have heaven as its source (see D&C 50:13–20), and it is to "descend" upon us "as the dews of Carmel" (D&C 128:19; see also 121:45). It is the knowledge that has been hidden from the world (see D&C 124:41) that rises with us in the resurrection. It is a knowledge obtained only in the classrooms of "diligence and obedience" (D&C 130:19). Such was the classroom in which Christ gained his testimony, and such is the classroom in which we must gain our testimonies.

NOTES

1. Smith, *Teachings*, 220.

2. Leon-Dufour, *Dictionary of the New Testament*, 259; emphasis added.

3. Richards, *Expository Dictionary of Bible Words*, 386.

CHAPTER 18

WITH CHRIST, WE WORSHIP THE FATHER

A CLEAR understanding of the relationship between the Father and the Son is essential to a testimony that has the power of salvation in it. As Latter-day Saints our testimony is that Jesus of Nazareth is the actual and literal Son of God. Where scripture speaks of God as his "Father," we accept it in the plain and direct meaning of the word. We believe the word "father" to mean "father," the word "son" to mean "son," and the word "begotten" to mean "begotten." We believe Christ to be the creation of his divine Father and his mortal mother, Mary. He is their child in the same sense that I am the child of my parents and you are the child of your parents. We believe that Christ came to the earth to work out his own salvation and to make salvation possible for all the kindred of God through an atoning sacrifice that would free them from all the effects of Adam's fall on condition of their repentance.

The concept that Christ needed to work out his own salvation has not been taught as well as it ought to have been. Joseph Smith, however, taught the principle with considerable clarity. In *Lectures on Faith* he wrote:

Where shall we find a prototype into whose likeness we may be assimilated, in order that we may be made partakers of life and salvation? Or in other words, where shall we find a saved being? For if we can find a saved being, we may ascertain without much difficulty, what all others must be in order to be saved. They must be like that individual or they cannot be saved. We think that it will not be a matter of dispute, that two beings who are unlike each other cannot both be saved; for whatever constitutes the salvation of one, will constitute the salvation of every creature which will be saved. And if we find one saved being in all existence, we may see what all others must be, or else not be saved We ask then, where is the prototype? Or where is the saved being? We conclude as to the answer of this question there will be no dispute among those who believe the Bible, that it is Christ. All will agree in this that he is the prototype or standard of salvation, or in other words that he is a saved being. And if we should continue our interrogation, and ask how it is that he is saved, the answer would be because he is a just and holy being; and if he were anything different from what he is, he would not be saved; for his salvation depends on his being precisely what he is and nothing else; for if it were possible for him to change in the least degree, so sure he would fail of salvation and lose all his dominion, power, authority, and glory—which constitutes salvation; for salvation consists in the glory, authority, majesty, power, and dominion which Jehovah possesses, and in nothing else; and no being can possess it but himself or one like him. Thus says John in his first epistle, 3:2–3, "Beloved, now are we the sons of God, and it doth not yet appear what we shall be: but we know that, when he shall appear, we shall be like him: for we shall see him as he is. And every man that hath this hope in him, purifieth himself, even as he is pure." Why purify himself as he is pure? Because, if they do not, they cannot be like him.[1]

CHRIST TAUGHT US TO WORSHIP THE FATHER

The system of worship taught to us by Christ was that we worship the Father. We do so by embracing the plan of salvation instituted by the Father in the grand councils of heaven. It is to the Father that we pray, and it is from the Father that Christ came as "the messenger of the covenant," or "messenger of salvation" (Malachi 3:1; D&C 93:8). The first words recorded from the lips of the Savior during his mortal ministry are found in the book of Luke, when he as a twelve-year-old boy was found teaching in the temple. To anxious parents who thought him lost he simply said, "Wist ye not that I must be about my Father's business?" (Luke 2:49). The last words to fall from his lips as he hung upon the cross were "Father, into thy hands I commend my spirit: and having said thus, he gave up the ghost" (Luke 23:46). All that he taught between those two statements had as its purpose to center our attention on the Father and that which was necessary for us to do to return to his presence. Christ came in the name of the Father and as the messenger of the Father. To illustrate the emphasis that Christ placed on seeking to please the Father in all things in his personal worship, let us take twelve out of the more than one hundred expressions he made to that effect in the Gospel of John.

"Jesus saith unto them, My meat is to do the will of him that sent me, and to finish his work" (John 4:34).

"Verily, verily, I say unto you, He that heareth my word, and believeth on him that and sent me, hath everlasting life" (John 5:24).

"I can of mine own self do nothing: as I hear, I judge: and my judgment is just; because I seek not mine own will, but the will of the Father which hath sent me" (John 5:30).

"For the works which the Father hath given me to finish, the same works that I do, bear witness of me, that the Father hath sent me" (John 5:36).

"Jesus answered and said unto them, This is the work of God, that ye believe on him whom he hath sent" (John 6:29).

"Jesus answered them, and said, My doctrine is not mine, but his that sent me. If any man will do his will, he shall know of the doctrine, whether it be of God, or whether I speak of myself" (John 7:16–17).

"Jesus said unto them, If God were your Father, ye would love me: for I proceeded forth and came from God; neither came I of myself, but he sent me" (John 8:42).

"I must work the works of him that sent me" (John 9:4).

"Jesus cried and said, He that believeth on me, believeth not on me, but on him that sent me" (John 12:44).

"For I have not spoken of myself; but the Father which sent me, he gave me a commandment, what I should say, and what I should speak" (John 12:49).

"Verily, verily, I say unto you, the servant is not greater than his lord; neither he that is sent greater than he that sent him" (John 13:16).

"He that loveth me not keepeth not my sayings: and the word which ye hear is not mine, but the Father's which sent me" (John 14:24).

As would be expected, the Book of Mormon evidences Christ's loyalty to this same principle while extending our understanding of it. From the Book of Mormon we learn that the principle here involved reminds unchanged with the resurrected and exalted Christ. Introducing himself to the Nephites at the temple in Bountiful he said: "Behold, verily, verily, I say unto you I will declare unto you my doctrine. And this is my doctrine, and it is the doctrine which the Father hath given unto me; and I bear record of the Father, and the Father beareth record of me, and the Holy Ghost beareth record of the Father and me; and I bear record that the Father commandeth all men, everywhere, to repent and believe in me" (3 Nephi 11:31–32).

Brief accounts are given of two prayers Christ offered while he visited among the Nephites. They illustrate that exalted beings are not above and beyond the need to worship and pray, just as they did before they were resurrected.

> Behold he prayed unto the Father, and the things which he prayed cannot be written, and the multitude did bear record who heard him. And after this manner do they bear record: The eye hath never seen, neither hath the ear heard, before, so great and marvelous things as we saw and heard Jesus speak unto the Father; and no tongue can speak, neither can there be written by any man, neither can the hearts of men conceive so great and marvelous things as we both saw and heard Jesus speak; and no one can conceive of the joy which filled our souls at the time we heard him pray for us unto the Father (3 Nephi 17:15–17).

From the prayer offered by Christ on the following day we read this expression: "Father, I thank thee that thou hast purified those whom I have chosen, because of their faith, and I pray for them, and also for them who shall believe on their words, that they may be purified in me, through faith on their words, even as they are purified in me. Father, I pray not for the world, but for those whom thou hast given me out of the world, because of their faith, that they may be purified in me, that I may be in them as thou, Father, art in me, that we may be one, that I may be glorified in them" (3 Nephi 19:28–29).

The Eternal Family Unit

It is profoundly important that we as Latter-day Saints recognize in the testimony that we bear that Christ is God's Son now and forever. The whole system and plan of salvation centers around the preservation of the family unit. God will always be God, and Christ will always be his Son. I will always be the son of my father, and I, through the covenants of the temple, will have claim to the companionship and love of my wife and children. We cannot, as the traditional Christian world has done, compound the personages of the Father and the Son, supposing them to be one and the same, without at the same time losing the entire plan of salvation. The power of salvation is not found in figurative truths but in the reality of a literal resurrection that inseparably unites flesh and bone, preserves gender, and grants the power of procreation. All such truths and a thousand more are lost when the knowledge of the fatherhood of God and the divine sonship of Christ are lost.

Surely it was for this reason that both the Father and the Son appeared to Joseph Smith in the Sacred Grove to answer his question as to which church he should join. The church Joseph sought must be founded on eternal truth. It must begin with the restoration of a correct understanding of the nature of God and our relationship to him. Thus, as the heavens were opened to introduce this final great gospel dispensation, the foundational truth that the Father and the Son are separate and distinct and that the Son acts under the direction of the Father were clearly manifest. It follows most naturally that the founding document of Mormonism invites us to stand before the whole world and declare that God both speaks again and manifests himself to men in the flesh, declaring:

> By these things [that is, the First Vision and the Book of Mormon] we know that there is a God in heaven, who is infinite and eternal, from everlasting to everlasting the same unchangeable God, the framer of heaven and earth, and all things which are in them; and that he created man, male and female, after his own image and in his own likeness, created he them; and gave unto them commandments that they should love and serve him, the only living and true God, and that he should be the only being whom they should worship. (D&C 20:17–19)

So it is that we reject the theological rubble upon which the traditional Christian world has rested its hope of salvation since that day long ago when the plain reading of the gospel text was abandoned for a God who is incomprehensible and unknowable.

ALL THE PROPHETS SO TESTIFIED

As Latter-day Saints, in concert with all the holy prophets, we worship the Father, not the Son, not the Holy Ghost, not holy angels, not specially chosen saints. We worship the Father and we do it in the name of Christ, for so the Father commanded and so Christ taught and so the scriptures direct. Speaking of the ancient prophets, Jacob, son of Lehi, declared, "Behold, they [all the prophets before him] believed in Christ and worshiped the Father in his name, and also we worship the Father in his name" (Jacob 4:5). Again, we read that the voice of the Lord to Moses from the burning bush was, "Call upon God in the name of mine Only Begotten, and worship me" (Moses 1:17). To the woman at the well in Samaria, Christ said, "Ye worship ye know not what: we know what we worship: for salvation is of the Jews. But the hour cometh, and now is, when the true worshippers shall worship the Father in spirit and in truth: for the Father seeketh such to worship him" (John 4:22–23). Returning to our dispensation, the founding document of Mormonism states, "And we know that all men must repent and believe on the name of Jesus Christ, and worship the Father in his name, and endure in faith on his name to the end, or they cannot be saved in the kingdom of God" (D&C 20:29).

Thus we testify that Jesus of Nazareth is the Firstborn Son of the Father and that he faithfully did the will of his Father in all things, and that in and through his atoning sacrifice he became the Savior to all his Father's children. We know and understand that if it were not for his atoning sacrifice we could not be saved. In making that sacrifice, Christ was doing the will of the Father and filling a covenant he made with our Eternal Father in the councils of heaven long before the earth was created. Having presented his plan for our salvation in the heavenly council, the Father explained the necessity of one coming to perform an atoning sacrifice and asked, "Whom shall I send?" Christ answered, "Here am I, send me" (Abraham 3:27), and then added, "Thy will be done, and the glory be thine forever" (Moses 4:2). Having completed the atoning act, and just before he gave up the ghost, Christ addressed himself to the Father saying, "It is finished, thy will is done" (JST, Matthew 27:50).

THE FATHER, SON, AND HOLY GHOST ARE DISTINCT PERSONAGES

In the traditional Christian world there is no need to distinguish between the worship of Christ, his Father, or the Holy

Spirit, for they are believed to be of the same essence. The announcement that we as Latter-day Saints worship the Father, and not the Son and not the Holy Ghost, is greeted with shouts of heresy and is cited as evidence that we are not Christian. Thus this doctrine, as with all the other doctrines we have considered as part of our testimony of Christ, invites us to stand on our own ground and be true to our own principles. It also allows us to believe the plain meaning of hundreds of scriptural texts that otherwise are mystified to accord with the doctrine of the Holy Trinity.

Hundreds of passages of scripture in the Bible can be cited to sustain the verity that God and men are of the same race. Yet in response, *The Cambridge History of the Bible* states, "Eusebius is a faithful enough disciple of Origen to agree with Plato that it is sometimes necessary for the lawgiver to lie in order to persuade people rather than coerce them, and to suggest that this is an explanation of the anthropomorphism of the Old Testament."[2] And *The Oxford Dictionary of the Christian Church* explains that every plain and positive statement about God in scripture or in the sermons of the early Christian Fathers "are but metaphors devised for the ignorant."[3]

We certainly are not at odds with scriptural texts that declare the Godhead to be one. Indeed, the strongest expressions to this effect are found in the revelations of the Restoration. The same text cited above, which declares that the Father is the only being that we worship, states that the "Father, Son, and Holy Ghost are one God, infinite and eternal, without end" (D&C 20:28). The three members of the Godhead are being declared one to emphasize that in all things they are in perfect accord with each other. This is the most dramatic teaching device in all the eternities. God is one, and to obtain salvation we must become one with him.

To obtain salvation is to become one with God; it is to think as he thinks, believe as he believes, and to act as he would act.

To the extent that we do this, we are saved. To the extent that we differ from him or are unlike him, we remain unsaved. Salvation consists in our being in both the image and likeness of God, image having reference to his physical appearance and likeness referring to his nature. Adam and Eve were not created with the idea that they become as different as possible from their divine Creator but rather that his nature would become theirs. Peter described it as our being "partakers of the divine nature" (2 Peter 1:4); Paul spoke of it as our being "conformed to the image of his Son" (Romans 8:29); Alma spoke of our "having the image of God engraven upon [our] countenances" (Alma 5:19); Joseph Smith spoke of this as our being "assimilated" in to the likeness of God.[4] Thus the Lord himself said, "I say unto you, be one; and if ye are not one ye are not mine" (D&C 38:27).

CHRIST MARKS THE PATH

Christ marks the path to lead us back to his Father. We are told that Christ is the "way," the "path," the "door," and that no man can come unto the Father unless they follow the example or path marked out by him. Let us take the ordinance of baptism to illustrate the point. Christ was baptized to conform to the will of the Father so that he could enter into the kingdom of the God, that being the only gate or entrance into God's kingdom. It was also necessary for Christ to be baptized so that he might receive all the other saving ordinances of the gospel. Thus it was that after Christ had been baptized by water, the Holy Ghost fell upon him. This is the pattern established in heaven whereby that gift is given (see 2 Nephi 31:5–12).

Appropriately, the Lord has given us a revelation to tell us "what" we worship and "how" we worship. The revelation tells us that the "how" of worship is to advance from grace to grace as Christ did. The revelation illustrates that all professions of faith are meaningless unless we live in accordance with the laws and ordinances of the gospel. Thus Christ declared, "For if you keep my commandments you shall receive of his fulness, and be glorified in me as I am in the Father; therefore, I say unto you, you shall receive grace for grace" (D&C 93:20). True worship is measured in what we do and how we do it. Ours is a doing religion. It requires us to live and learn as Christ did to obtain the fulness of the Father (see D&C 93:6–19).

"And this is life eternal," Christ said, "that they might know thee the only true God, and Jesus Christ, whom thou hast sent" (John 17:3). The word *know* as used in this text is experiential, meaning that we know God only to the extent that we are like him, which is the extent to which we are one with him. Until we think as he thinks, believe as he believes, and do as he would do, we cannot be saved. One cannot isolate the gift of grace from the necessity of our walking the path marked by Christ, which path leads back to the presence of the Father. The whole system and plan of salvation centers around this principle.

Christ's purpose was to teach that there could be only one plan of salvation. The religious world today is filled with tens of thousands of variations of that plan. As prophesied, we have no shortage of false Christs or false plans of salvation. We can gain the fulness of the glory that Christ obtained only by obedience to the same principles to which he rendered complete obedience.

Christ As Our Mediator

All men are subject to the effects of the Fall; they are carnal, sensual, and devilish by nature. Thus as Paul says, "All things are of God, who hath reconciled us to himself by Jesus Christ, and hath given to us the ministry of reconciliation; to wit, that God was in Christ reconciling the world unto himself." We have "the word of reconciliation," which is found only in the gospel; thus our message is, "Be ye reconciled to God" (see 2 Corinthians 5:18–20).

Christ is the mediator between God and man. "Listen to him who is the advocate with the Father, who is pleading your cause before him—saying: Father, behold the sufferings and death of him who did no sin, in whom thou wast well pleased; behold the blood of my Son which was shed, the blood of him whom thou gavest that thyself might be glorified; wherefore, Father, spare these my brethren that believe on my name, that they may come unto me and have everlasting life" (D&C 45:3–5). Paul stated the matter thus: "There is one God, and one mediator between God and men, the man Christ Jesus; who gave himself a ransom for all" (1 Timothy 2:5–6). Such mediation is essential to the salvation of all who have been born into this fallen world.

Thus our testimony is that God stands "supreme, paramount, and pre-eminent" over all other created things.[5] He gave us life, and the agency to give it purpose and meaning. He gave us the plan of salvation, and it was he who sent his Only Begotten Son to the world to redeem us. Such is the faith that stands at the very heart of the testimony we bear. We have no doctrine that does not trace to the Father. All our doctrines take life from the knowledge that God is our divine Father, and all our doctrines would lose purpose and meaning should this doctrine be lost to our understanding.

WHO WE WORSHIP

Scripture commands that we worship only the Father; but the scriptures also speak of our worshiping Christ. Our response can be one of frustration, or we can acknowledge the limitations of language and conclude that there is an important difference in the way the word *worship* is being used in both instances. It is like the word *president* as we use it in the Church. No one supposes that the word *president* means exactly the same thing when they speak of a deacon's quorum president and the President of the Church; yet the word *president* is perfectly appropriate in both instances.

So let it be said that we "worship" Christ; to him we bow the knee, to him we prostrate ourselves upon the earth, with him we pray to the Father, and with him we worship the Father and seek to do the Father's will in all things.

Notes

1. Smith, *Lectures on Faith*, 7:9.
2. Ackroyd and Evans, *Cambridge History of the Bible*, 1:452.
3. Cross and Livingstone, *Oxford Dictionary of the Christian Church*, 576.
4. Smith, *Lectures on Faith*, 7:16.
5. McConkie, "Our Relationship with the Lord."

CHAPTER 19

TWO COMFORTERS

A<small>T</small> the Last Supper, as Christ prepared his Apostles for his departure, he promised them two comforters. The first was the companionship of the Holy Ghost, the full power of which had been constrained during Christ's mortal ministry. The Second Comforter was nothing less than the promise that he and his Father would come to bless and instruct them. "I will pray the Father," Christ said, "and he shall give you another Comforter, that he may abide with you for ever; even the Spirit of truth; whom the world cannot receive, because it seeth him not, neither knoweth him: but ye know him; for he dwelleth with you, and shall be in you" (John 14:16–17).

The title "Spirit of truth" can apply either to Christ or the Holy Ghost. In this text it applies to the companionship of the Holy Ghost, which the world cannot receive. Every accountable soul is entitled to the Light of Christ; the companionship of the Holy Ghost comes only after baptism and is the exclusive providence of Latter-day Saints. This is not to say that those in the world cannot experience manifestations from the Holy Ghost, but it is to say that they are not entitled to the constant light that is associated with it. The manifestations granted to them will always have as their purpose to prepare them for baptism and full fellowship with the Saints.

THE FIRST COMFORTER AND THE TIME OF CHRIST

It is common among Latter-day Saints to say that the Twelve did not enjoy the companionship of the Holy Ghost until after the ascension of Christ. The present text suggests that such a conclusion is not correct. "He dwelleth with you," Christ told them (John 14:17). Nephi testified that the "Holy Ghost" was "the gift of God unto all those who diligently seek him [meaning Christ], as well in times of old *as in the time that he should manifest himself unto the children of men* (1 Nephi 10:17; emphasis added). Luke specifically tells us that Simeon identified and testified of Christ by the power of the Holy Ghost, and undoubtedly Anna did also, for one cannot bear a competent witness of Christ independent of the sustaining power of the Holy Ghost (see Luke 2:25, 37–38).

After the bread of life sermon in Capernaum many of the followers of Christ chose to part company with him, causing Christ to turn to the Twelve and ask, "Will ye also go away? Then Simon Peter answered him, Lord, to whom shall we go? thou hast the words of eternal life. And we believe and are sure that thou art that Christ, the Son of the living God" (John 6:67–69). Again such a testimony cannot be borne independent of the sustaining power of the Holy Ghost.

This would be equally true of the testimony borne by Peter in Caesarea Philippi when Christ asked the Twelve whom they believed him to be. Again Peter is the spokesman, saying, "Thou art the Christ, the Son of the living God," to which Jesus responded, "Blessed art thou, Simon Bar-jona: for flesh and blood hath not revealed it unto thee, but my Father which is in heaven" (Matthew 16:16–17). Again, such revelation comes only from the Holy Ghost. Thus we have every confidence that the Twelve and all faithful followers of Christ knew him to be the Son of God by the power of the Holy Ghost, notwithstanding the fact that the First Comforter was limited or constrained during the mortal ministry of the Master.

A Second Comforter Also Promised

In addition to the companionship of the Holy Ghost, Christ also told the Twelve that "if a man love me, he will keep my words: and my Father will love him, and we will come unto him, and make our abode with him" (John 14:23). Commenting on this verse, Joseph Smith said, "John 14:23—The appearing of the Father and the Son, in that verse, is a personal appearance; and the idea that the Father and the Son dwell in a man's heart is an old sectarian notion, and is false" (D&C 130:3). Further explaining the words of Christ, the Prophet said:

> There are two Comforters spoken of. One is the Holy Ghost, the same as given on the day of Pentecost, and that all Saints receive after faith, repentance, and baptism. This first Comforter or Holy Ghost has no other effect than pure intelligence. It is more powerful in expanding the mind, enlightening the understanding, and storing the intellect with present knowledge, of a man who is of the literal seed of Abraham, than one that is a Gentile, though it may not have half as much visible effect upon the body; for as the Holy Ghost falls upon one of the literal seed of Abraham, it is calm and serene; and his whole soul and body are only exercised by the pure

spirit of intelligence; while the effect of the Holy Ghost upon a Gentile, is to purge out the old blood, and make him actually of the seed of Abraham. That man that has none of the blood of Abraham (naturally) must have a new creation by the Holy Ghost. In such a case, there may be more of a powerful effect upon the body, and visible to the eye, than upon an Israelite, while the Israelite at first might be far before the Gentile in pure intelligence.

The other Comforter spoken of is a subject of great interest, and perhaps understood by few of this generation. After a person has faith in Christ, repents of his sins, and is baptized for the remission of his sins and receives the Holy Ghost, (by the laying on of hands), which is the first Comforter, then let him continue to humble himself before God, hungering and thirsting after righteousness, and living by every word of God, and the Lord will soon say unto him, Son, thou shalt be exalted.

When the Lord has thoroughly proved him, and finds that the man is determined to serve Him at all hazards, then the man will find his calling and his election made sure, then it will be his privilege to receive the other Comforter, which the Lord hath promised the Saints, as is recorded in the testimony of St. John, in the 14th chapter, from the 12th to the 27th verses.

Having then quoted those verses the Prophet continues his discussion, asking,

Now what is this other Comforter? It is no more nor less than the Lord Jesus Christ Himself; and this is the sum and substance of the whole matter; that when any man obtains this last Comforter, he will have the personage of Jesus Christ to attend him, or appear unto him from time to time, and even He will manifest the Father unto him, and they will take up their abode with him, and the visions of the heavens will be opened unto him, and the Lord will teach him face to face, and he may have a perfect knowledge of the mysteries of the Kingdom of God; and this is the state and place the ancient Saints arrived at when they had such glorious visions—Isaiah, Ezekiel, John upon the Isle of Patmos, St. Paul in the three heavens, and all the Saints who held communion with the general assembly and Church of the Firstborn.[1]

Promises Given the Saints

While the blessings associated with the Second Comforter are exclusive to those who have obtained great spiritual maturity, the promise is extended to all who are numbered among the household of faith. It is within our capacity to obtain such blessings. This promise finds frequent mention in the revelations of the Restoration.

Doctrine and Covenants 93:1 states that "every soul who forsaketh his sins and cometh unto me, and calleth on my name, and obeyeth my voice, and keepeth my commandments, shall see my face and know that I am." We would understand this to apply to this life, and not simply the world to come.

Our revelations on the Melchizedek Priesthood tell us that it was restored in order that the children of God might once again be brought into the divine presence. It is not future worlds to which this promise is directed but to the mortal and corruptible state in which we now reside. The ordinances (rites or rituals) of the priesthood are designed to prepare both men and woman to stand in the presence of God while in the flesh (see D&C 84:19–25; 107:18–19).

Of Joseph Smith's vision on the degrees of glory, we are told that all who love the Lord and purify themselves are entitled to receive the same vision. Of these the Lord says, "To whom he grants this privilege of seeing and knowing for themselves; that through the power and manifestation of the Spirit, while in the flesh, they may be able to bear his presence in the world of glory" (D&C 76:117–18). As this revelation begins we are told that all who fear God, meaning all who are properly reverential, and who serve him in righteousness and truth, will have the visions of eternity opened to them. "To them," the revelation states,

> will I reveal all mysteries, yea, all the hidden mysteries of my kingdom from days of old, and for ages to come, will I make known unto them the good pleasure of my will concerning all things pertaining to my kingdom.
>
> Yea, even the wonders of eternity shall they know, and things to come will I show them, even the things of many generations.
>
> And their wisdom shall be great, and their understanding reach to heaven; and before them the wisdom of the wise shall perish, and the understanding of the prudent shall come to naught.
>
> For by my Spirit will I enlighten them, and by my power will I make known unto them the secrets of my will—yea, even those things which eye has not seen, nor ear heard, nor yet entered into the heart of man. (D&C 76:7–10)

Similarly, the Lord asked, "What power shall stay the heavens? As well might man stretch forth his puny arm to stop the Missouri river in its decreed course, or to turn it up stream, as to hinder the Almighty from pouring down knowledge from heaven upon the heads of the Latter-day Saints" (D&C 121:33).

One could not find a sharper contrast in doctrines between such statements and promises and the professions of the traditional Christian world, which claims that all we can know is contained in the Bible as we now have it and that if it is not in the Bible we cannot know it.

How apt the words found in our hymn "Come, Listen to a Prophet's Voice":

Then heed the words of truth and light
That flow from fountains pure.
Yea, keep His law with all thy might
Till thine election's sure,
Till thou shalt hear the holy voice
Assure eternal reign,
While joy and cheer attend thy choice,
As one who shall obtain.[2]

NOTES

1. Smith, *Teachings,* 149–51.
2. *Hymns,* 21.

CHAPTER 20

THE GATHERING TO CHRIST

THE single most important sign of the times is the extent to which Israel has been gathered or the gospel taught among the nations of the earth. This event is entirely Christ centered. The gathering comes in answer to the scattering. When those of the house of Israel in ancient days rejected Christ, his prophets, and their covenants, they forfeited their right to lands of promise and were scattered throughout all the nations of the earth. They lost the knowledge of their chosen place as the agents of the Lord in teaching the gospel to all who were born outside the covenant. The Lord promised their fathers that in the last days they would be gathered again, meaning that they would return to a true knowledge and testimony of Christ, to following the words of his prophets, and to the saving ordinances and covenants God made with their fathers.

With the restoration of the gospel the gathering begins anew; people who have lost the knowledge of the promises God made to their ancient fathers have that knowledge restored to them, along with the covenants of salvation. In and through these covenants they come to a knowledge of Christ that can be had in no other way. Let us briefly review principles associated with this, the greatest saga in earth's history, and how it shapes our testimony of Christ.

LOCATING THE LOST TRIBES

In the most complete and proper sense, Israel has been gathered to the extent that her sons and daughters have returned to the house of the Lord and there entered into the same covenants that God made with Abraham, Isaac, and Jacob. The gathering begins at the time of their baptism, when they covenant to take upon themselves the name of Christ. It includes having a patriarch, rightfully called, lay his hands upon their heads and declare by the spirit of revelation their lineage among the tribes of Israel. This, then, means for the most part that Israel is still in a lost and fallen state and that the scattering continues as so many of Abraham's kin wander in spiritual darkness. If we are to understand this doctrine, we will be well served to set aside the myths of an earlier era and turn our attention to a careful consideration of the testimony of scripture. Perhaps this can best be done in question-and-answer format.

Question: Which tribes are still lost?

Answer: The more part of all twelve tribes.

Question: What does it mean to be lost? Does it mean that their whereabouts have been lost to us, or does it simply mean that they have lost their identity as the children of the covenant?

Answer: It means that they have lost the knowledge of the system and plan of salvation, that they do not know where to find the truth about Christ and the saving ordinances of his gospel.

Question: Are you saying that they are not hidden in a group somewhere or hidden under the polar ice cap?

Answer: Yes. We have hundreds of passages of scripture that tell us that people of all twelve tribes would be scattered throughout the whole earth and that they would be found among all nations.

Question: Could you show me a few of these passages?

Answer: Certainly. Nephi tells us that at the time the Book of Mormon comes forth "the Lord will set his hand again the second time to restore his people from their lost and fallen state" (2 Nephi 25:17). I do not think this was intended to mean that they could not be located on a map, that we did not know their longitude and latitude, but rather that they had lost the knowledge of who they were, what promises the Lord had made with them, and the saving truths about Christ. They are lost in the sense that they are in a state of ignorance where gospel truths are concerned.

The scriptures consistently promise that all the remnants of Jacob, meaning all twelve tribes, will be gathered all over the earth. For instance:

"I will bring thy seed from the east, and gather thee from the west; I will say to the north, Give up; and to the south, Keep not back: bring my sons from far, and my daughters from the ends of the earth" (Isaiah 43:5–6).

"And as surely as the Lord liveth, will he gather in from the four quarters of the earth all the remnant of the seed of Jacob, who are scattered abroad upon all the face of the earth" (3 Nephi 5:24).

"And then shall the remnants, which shall be scattered abroad upon the face of the earth, be gathered in from the east and from the west, and from the south and from the north; and they shall be brought to the knowledge of the Lord their God, who hath redeemed them" (3 Nephi 20:13).

"Yea, then will he remember the isles of the sea; yea, and all the people who are of the house of Israel, will I gather in, saith the Lord, according to the words of the prophet Zenos, from the four quarters of the earth" (1 Nephi 19:16).

"And even so will I gather mine elect from the four quarters of the earth, even as many as will believe in me, and hearken unto my voice" (D&C 33:6).

"And the saints shall come forth from the four quarters of the earth" (D&C 45:46).

Question: Is there a single great key to the gathering?

Answer: Yes. The Book of Mormon was ordained in the councils of heaven to be the book that gathered Israel or restored the great truths about Christ and his gospel that had been lost to them. If you will remember, the title page of the Book of Mormon states that it was written "to show unto the remnant of the House of Israel what great things the Lord hath done for their fathers; and that they may known the covenants of the Lord." When they come to this knowledge, they can then come to a true understanding of Christ and his saving ministry.

Question: It seems strange to me that you would say that a knowledge of the covenants comes before the testimony of Christ. Would you not have to believe in Christ before you entered into a covenant with him?

Answer: Yes, you would. What you are being told here is that the great testimony of Christ, the testimony that has the power of salvation in it, comes through the ordinances. Consider these words of Nephi: "And at that day shall the remnant of our seed know that they are of the house of Israel, and that they are the covenant people of the Lord; *and then* shall they know and come to the knowledge of their forefathers, and also to the knowledge of the gospel of their Redeemer, which was ministered unto their fathers by him; wherefore, they shall come to the knowledge of their Redeemer and the very points of his doctrine, that they may know how to come unto him and be saved" (1 Nephi 15:14; emphasis added).

Question: Are you saying that Israel cannot be gathered unless they join the Church?

Answer: I am. Nephi said it thus, "Yea, at that day, will they not receive the strength and nourishment from the true vine? Yea, will they not come unto the true fold of God?" (1 Nephi 15:15). Again he said, "They shall be restored to the true church and fold of God," and then they can be restored "to the lands of their inheritance" (2 Nephi 9:2). Christ put it this way, "If they will repent and hearken unto my words, and harden not their hearts, I will establish my church among them, and they shall come in unto the covenant and be numbered among this the remnant of Jacob" (3 Nephi 21:22).

Question: I thought our scriptures said that they would come back in a group with their prophets leading them?

Answer: The text you are referring to is found in Doctrine and Covenants 133 and is generally poorly read. It begins with the announcement that "the Lord, even the Savior, shall stand in the midst of his people, and shall reign over all flesh" (v. 25) which suggests that this will be a millennial event. (This does not suggest that the various quorums of the priesthood will be excused from the responsibilities that are theirs; missionaries will still be sent forth and the great labor of our temples will still continue.) Our text then says, "And they who are in the north countries shall come in remembrance before the Lord; and their prophets [prophets called and ordained under the hands of the president of The Church of Jesus Christ of Latter-day Saints] shall hear his voice, and shall no longer stay themselves; and they shall smite the rocks, and the ice shall flow down at their presence. And an highway shall be cast up in the midst of the great deep" (D&C 133:26–27).

The highway is identified by Isaiah in his language,

> And an highway shall be there, and a way, and it shall be called The way of holiness; the unclean shall not pass over it; but it shall be for those: the wayfaring men, though fools, shall not err therein. No lion shall be there, nor any ravenous beast shall go up thereon, it shall not be found there; but the redeemed shall walk there: and the ransomed of the Lord shall return, and come to Zion with songs and everlasting joy upon their heads: they shall obtain joy and gladness, and sorrow and sighing shall flee away. (Isaiah 35:8–10)

It is not a superhighway that we read of here, but rather the straight and narrow path.

If we are to be true to scripture, we need to understand that this event will take place under the direction of the man who stands at the head of the Church and kingdom of God and who holds the keys of the gathering of Israel and the leading of the ten tribes from the lands of the north.

Question: Doesn't that text also say that when they return they will bring their scriptures with them?

Answer: What it says is that "they shall bring forth their rich treasures unto the children of Ephraim, my servants" (D&C 133:30). At some point someone suggested that this meant scriptures, and people have been repeating it ever since. The greater probability is that it means what it says. By revelation Joseph Smith recorded the following:

204

And again, verily I say unto you, let all my saints come from afar. And send ye swift messengers, yea, chosen messengers, and say unto them: Come ye, with all your gold, and your silver, and your precious stones, and with all your antiquities; and with all who have knowledge of antiquities, that will come, may come, and bring the box-tree, and the fir-tree, and the pine-tree, together with all the precious trees of the earth; and with iron, with copper, and with brass, and with zinc, and with all your precious things of the earth; and build a house to my name, for the Most High to dwell therein. (D&C 124:25–27)

Question: Am I correct in concluding that this text is telling us that they are already members of the Church?

Answer: You are correct, and that means that their scriptures are the same as ours—the Bible, Book of Mormon, Doctrine and Covenants, and the Pearl of Great Price. We get scripture through the channels the Lord ordained, not from those not of our faith.

GATHERING ISRAEL MUST FIRST RETURN TO CHRIST

Question: Can anyone have claim upon a land of inheritance without having first returned to Christ?

Answer: No. Let me comply with the law of witnesses by inviting three of the ancient prophets to respond.

Jacob stated the matter thus: "Wherefore, after they are driven to and fro, for thus saith the angel, many shall be afflicted in the flesh, and shall not be suffered to perish, because of the prayers of the faithful; they shall be scattered, and smitten, and hated; nevertheless, the Lord will be merciful unto them, that *when* they shall come to the knowledge of their Redeemer, they shall be gathered together again to the lands of their inheritance" (2 Nephi 6:11; emphasis added).

Nephi, speaking words given by the Lord, wrote as follows:

> But behold, thus saith the Lord God: When the day cometh that they shall believe in me, that I am Christ, *then have I covenanted with their fathers that they shall be restored in the flesh, upon the earth, unto the lands of their inheritance. And it shall come to pass that they shall be gathered in from their long dispersion, from the isles of the sea, and from the four parts of the earth;* and the nations of the Gentiles shall be great in the eyes of me, saith God, in carrying them forth to the lands of their inheritance (2 Nephi 10:7–8; emphasis added)

Again Nephi said,

> And after they have been scattered, and the Lord God hath scourged them by other nations for the space of many generations, yea, even down from generation to generation until they shall be persuaded to believe in Christ, the Son of God, and the atonement, which is infinite for all mankind—and when that day shall come that they shall believe in Christ, and worship the Father in his name, with pure hearts and clean hands, and look not forward any more for another Messiah, then, at that time, the day will come that it must needs be expedient that they should believe these things. And the Lord will set his hand again the second time to restore his people from their lost and fallen state. Wherefore, he will proceed to do a marvelous work and a wonder among the children of men. (2 Nephi 25:16–17)

Mormon added his testimony in these words:

Yea, and surely shall he again bring a remnant of the seed of Joseph to the knowledge of the Lord their God. And as surely as the Lord liveth, will he gather in from the four quarters of the earth all the remnant of the seed of Jacob, who are scattered abroad upon all the face of the earth. And as he hath covenanted with all the house of Jacob, even so shall the covenant wherewith he hath covenanted with the house of Jacob be fulfilled in his own due time, unto the restoring all the house of Jacob unto the knowledge of the covenant that he hath covenanted with them. *And then shall they know their Redeemer, who is Jesus Christ, the Son of God; and then shall they be gathered in from the four quarters of the earth unto their own lands, from whence they have been dispersed;* yea, as the Lord liveth so shall it be. Amen. (3 Nephi 5:23–26; emphasis added)

This may well be the most emphatic text in all of holy writ. I know of no other place were the text both begins and ends with the declaration that if God lives this must be so. It then states as plainly as language allows that Israel is scattered among all the nations of the earth and must return to Christ before she has any claim upon a land of inheritance.

The Gathering and the Priesthood

The gathering of Israel cannot take place independent of the restored priesthood and the ordinances thereof. In a revelation that continues the pattern of question and answers, we read the following:

"Questions by Elias Higbee: What is meant by the command in Isaiah, 52d chapter, 1st verse, which saith: Put on thy strength, O Zion—and what people had Isaiah reference to?"

Answer: "He had reference to those whom God should call in the last days, who should hold the power of priesthood to bring again Zion, and the redemption of Israel; and to put on her strength is to put on the authority of the priesthood, which she, Zion, has a right to by lineage; also to return to that power which she had lost" (D&C 113:7–8). The text clearly states that Zion cannot be established or Israel redeemed independent of the restored priesthood.

Question: "What are we to understand by Zion loosing herself from the bands of her neck; 2d verse?"

Answer: "We are to understand that the scattered remnants are exhorted to return to the Lord from whence they have fallen; which if they do, the promise of the Lord is that he will speak to them, or give them revelation. See the 6th, 7th, and 8th verses. The bands of her neck are the curses of God upon her, or the remnants of Israel in their scattered condition among the Gentiles" (D&C 113:9–10).

Question: It seems that these and the other texts you have quoted make it plain that the gathering of Israel in the present state of Israel do not represent the fulfillment of the gathering passages as found in the Book of Mormon and the Doctrine and Covenants.

Answer: That is correct. What is taking place in the state of Israel is a political gathering, not a spiritual gathering. It could be thought of as a precursor to the fulfillment of the kind of prophecies we are reading, but nothing more than that.

Question: I had always thought that God gave the Jews the Holy Land as their birthright. Is my understanding correct?

Answer: We read the following in the book of Abraham, "But, I, Abraham, and Lot, my brother's son, prayed unto the Lord, and the Lord appeared unto me, and said unto me: Arise, and take Lot with thee; for I have purposed to take thee away out of Haran, and to make of thee a minister *to bear my name* in a strange land which I will give unto thy seed after thee for an everlasting possession, *when they hearken to my voice"* (Abraham 2:6; emphasis added). The promise to a land of inheritance came in the form of a covenant between Abraham and Jehovah or Christ, whose name Abraham had taken upon himself. His seed were to be rightful heirs to that land as long as they were faithful to Christ. There is no promise to a land of inheritance independent of faith in Christ. Thus neither Jew nor Arab have any claim to the land on the basis of the covenant God made with Abraham.

Returning to the point of our beginning, the single greatest sign of the times must be the extent to which the testimony of Christ, his Church, and his priesthood sweep the earth. Surely we could find no more dramatic illustration of the necessity of our having a clear understanding of how we differ in testimony from the traditional Christian world.

Chapter 21

Temples Testify
of Christ

From the beginning of time, everything associated with Israel's temple had as its purpose to testify of Christ. The temple known to the Old Testament was of the Aaronic or Levitical order; it was designed to house the performance of rituals associated with the Law of Moses. Everything in that law had as its purpose to prepare those living it to receive the Christ. Its system of worship centered on the law of sacrifice, in which a lamb of God was slain as an atonement for the sins of the people. Only the high priest, a type and shadow for Christ, could enter the holy place, and that alone on Yom Kippur, meaning "the day of atonement." No principle was better understood in ancient Israel than that no unclean thing could enter the presence of the Lord, and hence a purification ritual was required of those who entered the temple's inner courts. Before a priest could labor in the temple he had to go through a ritual washing and anointing, and then be clothed in the garments of the priesthood. Each of the thousand details associated with the little understood law given by revelation to Moses on Sinai had as its purpose to testify of Christ.

As it was with that temple, so it was with the temple built to administer the fulness of the gospel law as it was had by the faithful from the days of Adam to the time of Moses and as it was restored to the Prophet Joseph Smith. Every ordinance, every practice, all that took place or that now takes place in true temples of the Lord follows the same pattern and bears testimony to the same truths. Everything witnesses that Jesus is the Christ. Despite the objection of our critics and the charge that we are but a secret cult, all who enter the temple are required to be clean, meaning that they have followed the timeless pattern of temple worthiness known to those who labored in the temple described in scripture. Today, as in the days of Adam, those who enter the temple are taught the law of sacrifice and the necessity of obedience if one is to successfully pass through the veil and enter into the celestial realm and the presence of the Father.

EDEN: EARTH'S FIRST TEMPLE

In the temple we learn that Adam was the first to have the gospel of Jesus Christ. From the book of Abraham we learn that the ordinances of the temple have existed whenever the higher or holy priesthood has been on the earth. We also learn that Eden is a cloaked and veiled temple story and that the ordinances of the temple were known to "Seth, Noah, Melchizedek, Abraham, and all to whom the Priesthood was revealed" (Abraham Facsimile 2, figure 3).

The gospel pattern is everlastingly the same. Wherever true religion is to be found, the principle of revelation that is immediate to the day in which it is given and the people to whom it is given will also be found. Wherever revelation is found, the priesthood will immediately follow. Once the priesthood has been established, those holding the keys of the priesthood, that is, the right of presidency, will become the channel for those revelations given to direct the affairs of the Church and to direct the administration of the ordinances of salvation. This in turn will result in the divine command to build temples to house the most sacred of those ordinances. Conversely, when revelation is lost the priesthood will also be lost, and the place and purpose of temples will be lost also.

The temple is a stage on which we act out the plan of salvation. Christ is central to all that takes place there. We learn of his role in the creation. We learn the true story of the events of Eden and come to see the tree of life as the representation of Christ. It is in the Eden story that we learn that before Adam and Eve were required to leave their paradisiacal state following their transgression, God taught them the law of sacrifice. Having taught them this law, he clothed them in coats of skins that could have come from animals that had been sacrificed. This clothing was to serve as a constant reminder to them that in and through the blood of the Lamb all the effects of Adam's fall would be rectified. Thus it would be that they would find safety and protection in a fallen world through their faith in Christ.

In the temple we learn that all gospel ordinances become of efficacy and force in and through the Atonement of Christ. Indeed, the testimony of his atoning sacrifice becomes essential to our coming forth in the resurrection and being able to enter into the presence of our Father. We also learn of the importance of the family unit in the eternal scheme of things and the importance of our being bound together as husbands and wives and of having our children sealed to us. It is in the temple that we obtain the promises of exaltation, including the power of creation, in order that we, like Father Abraham, might enjoy eternal increase throughout the endless expanse of eternity.

The Abrahamic Covenant

Temple worship was known to none more completely than Abraham, the father of the faithful. Sacred ordinances and covenants require sacred space for their performance. The covenant of salvation as made by God with Father Abraham was restored for us in its most complete form in the book or writings of Abraham. It reads as follows:

> My name is Jehovah, and I know the end from the beginning; therefore my hand shall be over thee.
>
> And I will make of thee a great nation, and I will bless thee above measure, and make thy name great among all nations, and thou shalt be a blessing unto thy seed after thee, that in their hands they shall bear this ministry and Priesthood unto all nations;
>
> And I will bless them through thy name; for as many as receive this Gospel shall be called after thy name, and shall be accounted thy seed, and shall rise up and bless thee, as their father;
>
> And I will bless them that bless thee, and curse them that curse thee; and in thee (that is, in thy Priesthood) and in thy seed (that is, thy Priesthood), for I give unto thee a promise that this right shall continue in thee, and in thy seed after thee (that is to say, the literal seed, or the seed of the body) shall all the families of the earth be blessed, even with the blessings of the Gospel, which are the blessings of salvation, even of life eternal. (Abraham 2:8–11)

Such is the promise that is made anew with a man and a woman when they are bound together in an eternal union as husband and wife. The promise is that their family unit will be eternal and that their children, born under the terms of this covenant, will have the right to all the blessings of the gospel. Their sons will have the right to the priesthood and are expected to count themselves among the army of missionaries that go forth to bless all the earth with a knowledge of the new and everlasting covenant as that covenant has been restored in our day. They will be those called upon to minister in the name of Christ and teach the doctrines of salvation, inviting all who will worthily do so to join with Israel once again at the altar of God to receive the blessings of his holy house.

THE HOUSE OF THE LORD

Malachi, who refers to Christ as the "messenger of the covenant," tells that in the last days he will "suddenly come to his temple" (Malachi 3:1). Given that the temple is the place of covenant, it seems most natural that the "messenger of the covenant" would come there to meet those prepared to receive him. That is, he will appear to his own people in his own house to ready them for the events of the great and dreadful day. His people will be endowed with power from on high as they were in ancient days, and they will know the same blessings of his protective hand. Temples are most assuredly a sign of the true Church, and the doctrines and practices of such are an inseparable part of the testimony that the Lord's people have always been called on to bear to the nations of the earth.

Isaiah, describing the last days, spoke of gathering Israel coming from the ends of the earth to "the mountain of the Lord's house" to be instructed in the ways of the God of Jacob (Isaiah 2:2–3). What more perfect instruction could they receive than to be invited to enter into the same covenants and receive the same promises as did their ancient fathers, Abraham, Isaac, and Jacob?

All revelation given for the salvation of men in this world

comes from Christ and thus bears witness and testimony of him. Our temples are places of holiness and thus once dedicated are not open to the public. All who worthily enter a temple will "feel constrained" to acknowledge that it was sanctified and that it is a place of holiness (D&C 109:13). No unclean thing is permitted to enter the temple (see D&C 109:20). In the temple the faithful in Israel are endowed with power from on high, thus assuring them that they will be equal to the tasks the Lord has given them and that they will be able to live up to the terms and conditions of the covenants they have entered. They are clothed, as it were, with the powers of heaven and blessed with a capacity to represent the Lord, teach his gospel, and testify of him with greater power than that known among men.

Temples are the embodiment of the mount of the Lord's house. They are the place where heaven and earth meet. The Lord promised that the great day of his coming will be preceded by many appearances to his people in his temples. As has already been discussed, temples play an important part in the gathering of Israel. This is the reason that Moses took the children of Israel to Mount Sinai. Sinai was Israel's first temple. Here they were to sanctify themselves and stand in the presence of God. When they proved unwilling to do so, Moses and the greater priesthood were taken from them, and they were left to wander in the wilderness for forty years so that another generation could be raised up that would be permitted to enter their land of promise (see D&C 84:19–25). It is for the same purpose that Israel is gathered in this, the dispensation of the fulness of times. So it is that temples stand as a constant witness of our testimony of Christ and our covenant to be his people.

In our day Israel is gathered for the same purpose, to sanctify itself and prepare itself to stand in the presence of the Lord.

Rather than return to Sinai, Israel is now invited to return to temples, which are built to house the sacred ordinances that anciently were performed on the holy mountain. To ancient Israel the Lord said, "Now therefore, if ye will obey my voice indeed, and keep my covenant, then ye shall be a peculiar treasure unto me above all people: for all the earth is mine: and ye shall be unto me a kingdom of priests, and an holy nation" (Exodus 19:5–6). As it was anciently, so it is today. In the reading of this text be reminded that at that point there was no Aaronic or Lesser Priesthood; thus the reference to "priests" is to the office of a high priest in the Melchizedek Priesthood.

In the preceding chapter we reviewed texts containing the promise to the faithful of our day that they might see the Lord while in the flesh. It was for this purpose that Moses sought to sanctify his people, which blessing they refused. All of Israel might have seen the Lord had they been willing to do so, but only a few did. We know that Moses and Aaron, Nadab and Abihu, who were Aaron's sons, "and seventy of the elders of Israel . . . saw the God of Israel," while that privilege was lost to the rest of their kinsmen (Exodus 24:9–10).

It is the purpose of the Melchizedek Priesthood to prepare men to see God. Those who hold this priesthood "have the privilege of receiving the mysteries of the kingdom of heaven, to have the heavens opened unto them, to commune with the general assembly and church of the Firstborn, and to enjoy the communion and presence of God the Father, and Jesus the mediator of the new covenant" (D&C 107:19).

CONCLUSION

The truths of heaven never go unopposed. It has been the practice of the adversary in dispensations past to counterfeit true religion, and it was therefore common to find various forms of temple worship and the endowment ceremony among virtually all the nations of the earth. In our dispensation that has not been the case. The reason for this, it would appear, is that in our day false religion has rejected the principle of revelation. Since temples are houses of revelation, to counterfeit the temple would require conceding the fact that true religion requires revelation. Temples, in the true and scriptural sense, cannot exist where revelation does not exist. Elder Bruce R. McConkie stated the matter thus: "The inspired erection and proper use of temples is one of the great evidences of the divinity of the Lord's work. Without revelation they can neither be built nor used. Where there are temples, with the spirit of revelation resting upon those who administer therein, there the Lord's people will be found; where these are not, the Church and kingdom and the truth of heaven are not."[1] Without temples the full knowledge and testimony of Christ cannot be had.

NOTE

1.   McConkie, *Mormon Doctrine*, 781.

CHAPTER 22

THE VOICE OF WARNING

OF necessity, our testimony of Christ embraces the responsibility to warn against the false Christs and prophets that the Master himself said would be numerous in the last days. In so doing we seek to sit in judgment on no man. Such is not our commission. We do not arrogate the right to ourselves to say who is "Christian" and who is not, nor do we make any profession to be more loved of God than any of his other sons and daughters. We do, however, profess a commission given to us by him to share all that has been entrusted to us with any and all willing to listen.

We do so earnestly, seeking always to conduct ourselves as he conducted himself. We know that "the powers of heaven cannot be controlled nor handled only upon the principles of righteousness. That they may be conferred upon us, it is true; but when we undertake to cover our sins, or to gratify our pride, our vain ambition, or to exercise control or dominion or compulsion upon the souls of the children of men, in any degree of unrighteousness, behold, the heavens withdraw themselves; the Spirit of the Lord is grieved," and then that Spirit is withdrawn. Rather, we believe the gospel must go forth in a spirit of "gentleness and meekness, and by love unfeigned; by kindness, and pure knowledge, which shall greatly enlarge the soul without hypocrisy, and without guile" (D&C 121:36–37, 41–42). All of this is but to say that the gospel of Jesus Christ can only be taught in the Spirit of Jesus Christ.

ALL ARE TO BE WARNED

Many of the revelations given to Joseph Smith have been bound together in a volume known to us as the Doctrine and Covenants. In the preface, or first section, of that compilation we have what is know as "the voice of warning," in which the Lord identifies the specific truths that must be declared to and accepted by all nations if the calamities of the last days are to be avoided. These truths constitute the core of the testimony of Christ and his gospel that we have been commissioned to bear among all people. They begin with the announcement that God speaks and that the heavens have again been opened. This revelation, like those that follow, repeatedly picks up the language of the King James Bible to announce the fulfillment of the many prophecies relative to the last days that are found within its covers. This constitutes the most emphatic statement that could be made that Mormonism is not a rejection of the Bible but rather the affirmation of its veracity and truthfulness.

The first section of the Doctrine and Covenants begins by drawing upon a prophecy penned by Isaiah, which tells of a latter-day prophet through whom the Lord will speak to all nations. Two doctrines are identified by which this prophet is to be known among the nations of the earth. First, he will have been called in the councils of heaven before his birth; and second, he will have been known by name even before his birth (see

Isaiah 49:1–3). This prophet, in turn, is to call and commission others who will carry the message forth in order that "the voice of warning shall be unto all people, by the mouths of my disciples, whom I have chosen in these last days" (D&C 1:4).

These servants, we are told, are to go forth clothed in the power and authority of God with the assurance that no earthly power will be able "to stay them" or prevent their message from going forth. They are to speak in the name of the living God, declare the message of the Restoration among all men, and seal up the "unbelieving and rebellious" for "the day when the wrath of God shall be poured out upon the wicked without measure— unto the day when the Lord shall come to recompense unto every man according to his work, and measure to every man according to the measure which he has measured to his fellow man" (see D&C 1:5–10).

FUNDAMENTAL TRUTHS OF WHICH WE MUST TESTIFY

The testimony that we would raise in warning embraces principles that are plain and simple, principles immediately identifiable by the Spirit of truth. First, it is for us to declare that salvation cannot be found in principles that are false. The Christian world today consists of more than twenty-three thousand denominations. Every doctrine that they espouse will find its contradiction among their number. Many claim that the sincerity of the believer will counter this difficulty. The response is self-contradictory; salvation is found either in Christ or in sincerity, and if it be not Christ but sincerity, the enemies of Christ have certainly proven themselves sincere—would they not then have first claim upon the blessings of heaven? To deny the necessity of saving truths in the guise of ignorance that is sincere is a clever way to deny the necessity of the life and mission of Christ. As "the voice of warning" declares, there can be but one "true and living church upon the face of the whole earth" (D&C 1:30).

Given that the principles of the gospel are everlastingly the same, the arguments against them remain the same also. The manner in which Christ was rejected in the meridian of time constitutes the pattern for his rejection in our day. Christ was rejected by the established but corrupted orthodoxy. He was rejected by the use of scriptural arguments and as an offense to their unscriptural but much-loved traditions. In response to those using the Bible of their day to reject him, Christ said:

> Search the scriptures; for in them ye think ye have eternal life: and they are they which testify of me.
>
> And ye will not come to me, that ye might have life.
>
> I receive not honour from men.
>
> But I know you, that ye have not the love of God in you.
>
> I am come in my Father's name, and ye receive me not; if another shall come in his own name, him ye will receive.
>
> How can ye believe, which receive honour one of another, and seek not the honour that cometh from God only?
>
> Do not think that I will accuse you to the Father: there is one that accuseth you, even Moses, in whom ye trust.
>
> For had ye believed Moses, ye would have believed me: for he wrote of me.
>
> But if ye believe not his writings, how shall ye believe my words? (John 5:39–47)

Moses was a disciple of Christ. All that he did was directed at preparing a people to accept him. Thus the use of the writings of Moses to reject Christ would make Moses, not Christ, the accuser of the children of Israel. Christ and his disciples were accused of seeking to destroy the Bible prophecy when indeed they came to announce its fulfillment. Their message forced the people of their day to choose between their loyalty to their religious traditions and a living voice, the living Christ, and they overwhelmingly chose to sustain their traditions and silence the voice of heaven.

The story repeats itself in our day. The announcement that God speaks, that the heavens have been opened again, is rejected in the name of loyalty to a closed canon. Not only does modern Christianity reject living revelation or the very foundation upon which it was built, but it does so in the name of loyalty to creeds concocted after they declared the heavens sealed. The creeds have thus become the adversary to the Spirit of truth.

Our testimony, then, centers in the declaration of a God who speaks and of prophets who have been called to echo his words. It is the Bible pattern and thus the confirmation of the verity of the testimony of the Bible. As the revelation states:

> And the arm of the Lord shall be revealed; and the day cometh that they who will not hear the voice of the Lord, neither the voice of his servants, neither give heed to the words of the prophets and apostles, shall be cut off from among the people;
>
> For they have strayed from mine ordinances, and have broken mine everlasting covenant;
>
> They seek not the Lord to establish his righteousness, but every man walketh in his own way, and after the image of his own god, whose image is in the likeness of the world, and whose substance is that of an idol, which waxeth old and shall perish in Babylon, even Babylon the great, which shall fall. (D&C 1:14–16)

The declaration is most descriptive. Israel wanders in her lost and fallen state because she broke the "everlasting covenant" and sat in the councils of men to make her own gods. If she chooses not to hear the voice of God's servants as they go forth to gather Israel by heralding the message of the Restoration, she will forfeit her place among the children of the covenant. In order that the calamities prophesied not come upon the children of men, "the voice of warning" declares that the Father and the Son appeared to Joseph Smith in the Sacred Grove and commenced the great and final dispensation of the gospel. All this, according to the revelation, is in order that:

1. Every man might speak in the name of the Lord.
2. Faith might increase in the world.
3. The everlasting covenant might be established.
4. The fulness of the gospel might be proclaimed by the weak and the simple among all the nations of the earth.

The Seven Deadly Heresies of Modern Christianity

The key doctrines addressed in this revelation are seven in number. They respond to the most common and deadly of heresies common to traditional Christianity. They are as follows:

First is the response to the idea so often heard by our missionaries that it is not "what" you believe but "how" you believe that counts. Indeed, "what" you believe determines "how" you will believe. There can be no salvation found in false principles. Again, there is and can be only one "true and living church upon the face of the whole earth."

Second, the canon of scripture has not been sealed; revelation was never intended to cease. Whenever the Lord has had a people that he acknowledged as his own, he has spoken to them by revelation. Indeed, there is no true religion without revelation. God stands revealed or he remains forever unknown. We teach no doctrine that does not bear the label *revelation*. Any doctrine that does not bear this label is not our doctrine, and it does not have the power of salvation in it.

Third, the doctrine of a closed canon is intended to seal the lips of living prophets. A church without living prophets is not a living church. It is not and cannot be one and the same with the church as organized by Christ in New Testament times or among the peoples of the Old Testament. "We believe in the same organization that existed in the Primitive Church, namely, apostles, prophets, pastors, teachers, evangelists, and so forth" (Articles of Faith 1:6). As the dove was appointed in the councils of heaven to be the sign of the Holy Ghost, so prophets were appointed to be a sign of the true Church.

Fourth, those sent of God must be commissioned of God and must be able to demonstrate that they have been so commissioned. "We believe that a man must be called of God, by prophecy, and by the laying on of hands by those who are in authority, to preach the Gospel and administer in the ordinances thereof" (Articles of Faith 1:5). All arguments against the necessity of priesthood are arguments in favor of spiritual chaos. They are descriptive of a god who walks in crooked paths and knows not his own mind and will. They take from God the right to choose his own agents and suggest that salvation is a matter of negotiation rather than one of following the path he has marked out.

Fifth, "We believe that through the Atonement of Christ, all mankind may be saved, by obedience to the laws and ordinances of the Gospel" (Articles of Faith 1:3). The Lord's house is a house of order. It is from the word *order* that we get the words *ordain* and *ordinances*, which aid in keeping the Lord's house orderly. The Lord's people have always been a covenant-making people. The covenants and the authority to perform them are essential to the restoration of the gospel. No one can receive a remission of sins independent of the ordinance of baptism.

Sixth, the idea that it does not particularly matter what you choose to believe about Christ as long as you believe in Christ may not carry with it any particular urgency to share the testimony of Christ with others. If truth is not an issue, then whatever truth you hold in such a faith cannot really be of any particular importance. Of necessity, true religion assumes the obligation to take the message of salvation to those of every nation, kindred, tongue, and people. While the responsibility to declare the gospel rests primarily with those who hold the priesthood, all share in the responsibility to sustain these missionary efforts. Israel must be gathered, and that gathering is to the truths declared in the revelation we now address. It means that they must march with the great army of Israel in the path marked by living prophets, bounded by the ordinances of salvation and the covenants they have made. If we have found the truth, we must have the spirit of truth, and that spirit requires that we share all that we have found with all who have not yet found it.

Seventh, implicit in all that has been said is the fundamental truth that God our eternal Father is a personal being who created us in his image and likeness; that Jesus of Nazareth is actually and literally his Son, through whose atoning sacrifice made it possible for us to come forth from the grave in the morning of the first resurrection; and that the Holy Ghost is a personage of spirit ordained in the heavenly councils to be the great witness or testator of all heaven-sent truths. These simple truths, attested to by every word of scripture ever penned, stand at the same time at complete odds with the doctrine of deity as espoused in the creeds of men.

Declaring the Message

Each of these fundamental truths finds expression in the revelation titled "the voice of warning." In the context of missionary work, we do not go forth to argue or contend in their favor. We simply declare these truths and allow the Spirit to attest to the hearts and minds of the honest in heart that they represent true religion. Out of them grows a host of other truths, each sweet to the taste and satisfying to the soul. Light always begets light, and one truth yet another. Each principle has within it its own spirit and the evidence of its own truthfulness. This is the spirit by which it was revealed and by which it must be understood. It is by that same Spirit that we seek to testify of these things.

CHAPTER 23

THE LIVING CHRIST

OUR testimony of Christ reaches beyond accounts given of his ministry in scripture. We testify that he lives, that he speaks, and that he manifests himself to his people today as literally as he ever did in any ancient day. We profess the same faith, the same knowledge, and the same gifts and signs that existed among the ancients.

"When faith comes," Joseph Smith taught,

> it brings its train of attendants with it—apostles, prophets, evangelists, pastors, teachers, gifts, wisdom, knowledge, miracles, healings, tongues, interpretation of tongues, etc. All these appear when faith appears on the earth, and disappear when it disappears from the earth; for these are the effects of faith, and always have attended, and always will, attend it. For where faith is, there will the knowledge of God be also, with all things which pertain thereto—revelations, visions, and dreams, as well as every necessary thing, in order that the possessors of faith may be perfected, and obtain salvation.[1]

The Living Christ

Our dispensation began with the appearance of the Father and the Son to the youthful Joseph Smith in a secluded grove of trees in upstate New York in the spring of 1820. Describing that sublime experience the Prophet said, "I was enwrapped in a heavenly vision, and saw two glorious personages, who exactly resembled each other in features and likeness, surrounded with a brilliant light which eclipsed the sun at noon day."[2] "One of them spake unto me, calling me by name and said, pointing to the other—*This is My Beloved Son. Hear Him!*" (JS–H 1:17). Thus our dispensation began with the invitation to see and hear the Son of God.

Significantly, on other occasions when Christ appeared to Joseph Smith, the Prophet was not alone. Describing the events surrounding the restoration of the Aaronic Priesthood in May of 1829, Oliver Cowdery wrote, "We were wrapped in the vision of the Almighty!"[3] While laboring on the Joseph Smith Translation of the Bible, the Prophet and Sidney Rigdon had the heavens opened to them, of which experience they said, "And now, after the many testimonies which have been given of him, this is the testimony, last of all [meaning most recently], which we give of him: That he lives! For we saw him, even on the right hand of God; and we heard the voice bearing record that he is the Only Begotten of the Father—that by him, and through him, and of him, the worlds are and were created, and the inhabitants thereof are begotten sons and daughters unto God" (D&C 76:22–24).

And again on April 3, 1835, in the Kirtland Temple Joseph and Oliver recorded:

The veil was taken from our minds, and the eyes of our understanding were opened. We saw the Lord standing upon the breastwork of the pulpit, before us; and under his feet was a paved work of pure gold, in color like amber. His eyes were as a flame of fire; the hair of his head was white like the pure snow; his countenance shone above the brightness of the sun; and his voice was as the sound of the rushing of great waters, even the voice of Jehovah, saying: I am the first and the last; I am he who liveth, I am he who was slain; I am your advocate with the Father. (D&C 110:1–4)

THE VOICE OF REVELATION

Membership in the Church brings with it the responsibility to know by the spirit of revelation that Jesus is the Christ, the Son of the Living God. No testimony is complete without this knowledge, which can come only from the Holy Ghost. John so attested when he said that "the testimony of Jesus is the spirit of prophecy" (Revelation 19:10). In his preface to the Doctrine and Covenants, the Lord tells us that the Church was restored "that every man might speak in the name of God the Lord, even the Savior of the world; that faith also might increase in the earth; that mine everlasting covenant might be established; that the fulness of my gospel might be proclaimed by the weak and the simple unto the ends of the world, and before kings and rulers" (D&C 1:20–23).

The greatest evidence that God speaks in our day is that men have been commissioned again to speak in his name and by the power of his Spirit. We generally define priesthood as the power and authority to speak in the name of God. Consider the ordinance of baptism as an illustration. To perform this ordinance, one must be a priest in the Aaronic Priesthood or hold the Melchizedek Priesthood. The baptismal prayer has been given by revelation: "Having been commissioned of Jesus Christ, I baptize you in the name of the Father, and of the Son, and of the Holy

Ghost. Amen" (D&C 20:73). This means that a sixteen-year-old priest in the Aaronic Priesthood is being commissioned to speak in the first person for all three members of the Godhead. The thought is stunning, but such is the order of heaven.

As to the authority that rests with the Melchizedek Priesthood, consider this description of how that priesthood has been used in ages past.

> Every one being ordained after this order and calling should have power, by faith, to break mountains, to divide the seas, to dry up waters, to turn them out of their course; to put at defiance the armies of nations, to divide the earth, to break every band, to stand in the presence of God; to do all things according to his will, according to his command, subdue principalities and powers; and this by the will of the Son of God which was from before the foundation of the world. (JST, Genesis 14:30–31)

Such powers are unknown to the churches of the world except as they read about them in scripture given to another people at another time. Yet the authority and power herein described rests with every man who holds the higher or holy priesthood.

All within the Church Are Called to Speak in His Name

It should also be noted that every man, woman, and child in the Church has been commissioned to speak in the name of Christ. It is in his name that we pray, and in his name that we teach and preach the gospel. The importance of this principle is not well understood by many in the Church. Consider, for instance, this statement made to the Twelve relative to the reading of the Book of Mormon. "These words are not of men nor of man, but of me; wherefore, you shall testify they are of me and not of man; for it is my voice which speaketh them unto you; for they are given by my Spirit unto you, and by my power you can read them one to another; and save it were by my power you could not have them; wherefore, you can testify that you have heard my voice, and know my words" (D&C 18:34–36).

This promise was given in June of 1829. The Quorum of the Twelve were not called until February of 1836. Yet the promise was theirs that when they read scripture by the power of the Spirit, they were hearing the voice of the Lord and could so testify.

As this principle is true of those called to be special witnesses of the Lord, it applies in like manner to all who have the gift of the Holy Ghost. Surely we have the same obligation to read scripture by the same Spirit as do the Twelve, and surely we have the right and responsibility to join them in testifying of the truthfulness of that which we have read. Indeed, we have been instructed that "all things must be done in the name of Christ, whatsoever you do in the Spirit" (D&C 46:31). Now we cannot do this without the spirit of revelation resting on us, just as it is to rest on our leaders.

It is by way of commandment that we speak as Christ would, for by using his name we declare ourselves to be standing in his stead. To pray for what we ought not in the name of Christ is to take his name in vain. So it is in what we teach or preach. Our call is to declare his gospel in the manner that he presented it to us. It is not for us to add to it or to take from it. We have no right to declare personal opinions in his name or seek to be amusing or entertaining. What we do in his name must be what he would do and say. Again, to do otherwise is to use his name in vain.

In the first section of the Doctrine and Covenants the Lord introduces all that is to follow in subsequent revelations. Concluding this section he says, "What I the Lord have spoken, I have spoken, and I excuse not myself; and though the heavens and the earth pass away, my word shall not pass away, but shall all be fulfilled, whether by mine own voice or by the voice of my servants, it is the same" (D&C 1:38).

The text identifies the standard by which any who profess to be his servants must measure that which they say and do. A revelation given to the newly formed Church describing the role of the prophet and seer says, "For his word ye shall receive, as if from mine own mouth, in all patience and faith" (D&C 21:5). As servants of the Lord we do not assume the responsibility to speak by way of direction to the Church, nor do we assume the prerogative to speak for the Church. This simply is not our office and calling, and we have no right to suppose that the Spirit would sustain our so doing.

At the same time we do have the responsibility, as called and ordained in various capacities, to give inspired direction and leadership over the stewardship entrusted to us. Within the bounds of the office and call given us, the principles and responsibilities are the same as those that direct him who stands at the helm of the good ship Zion. We must fill our office with the same solemnity with which he fills his.

This principle finds illustration in the only scriptural definition we have of *scripture*. The text states, "And whatsoever they shall speak when moved upon by the Holy Ghost shall be scripture, shall be the will of the Lord, shall be the mind of the Lord, shall be the word of the Lord, shall be the voice of the Lord, and the power of God unto salvation" (D&C 68:4).

The responsibility to so act and so speak does not rest with the general officers of the Church alone. It belongs to everyone who has been directed by the power of the priesthood to receive the gift of the Holy Ghost. Without this gift we cannot be competent witnesses of Christ, nor can we possess the kind of testimony that has the power of salvation in it.

Notes

1. Smith, *Lectures on Faith*, 7:20.
2. Smith, *History of the Church*, 4:536.
3. Oliver Cowdery, *Messenger and Advocate*, October 1834, 15.

CHAPTER 24

THE RETURN OF CHRIST

OUR testimony of Christ most assuredly includes the sure promise of his return. From the time of his ascension from the Mount of Olives just east of Jerusalem to the present moment, those of faith have anxiously looked to the day of his promised return. He has come as the suffering servant who chose to descend below all things and suffer the pains of all men; because of his offering, those who truly follow him can enter once again into the presence of their divine Father. Now he is to come as Lord of lords and King of kings to take judgment on the wicked and cleanse the earth of all corruptible things, that he might rule and reign in the splendor of millennial glory.

As a Church and people, it is our responsibility to prepare the way for him, which we seek to do. In this great cause angels have been and will continue to be our companions. John the Baptist was to prepare the way for him in his mortal ministry, which he did by the power of testimony and through the ordinance of a new baptism. John has come the second time and restored that same authority, that we might once again lawfully and legally cleanse men of sin and prepare them to stand clean and pure in the presence of Christ their Lord and Master. In like manner, Elijah has also come a second time to restore the keys of the sealing power, according to the prophecy of Malachi. An impressive list of other prophets has also come, each to restore the keys, powers, and majesties that were theirs so we might enjoy the gospel in its fulness. Our missionaries go forth to the ends of the earth to declare the reality of the Restoration, and temples follow, bringing with them all the blessings and promises given to the faithful in ages past. Christ has visited the world of the spirits and turned the key so the prisoners might go free through the preaching of the gospel there and the performance of temple ordinances here. Thus the stage is set.

WHAT MUST YET BE DONE

Missionary work is yet in its infancy. To this point in the history of the Church, we have been able to reach out to a comparative few on this continent and in Europe. We have not as yet gone in strength to the great hosts in Africa, India, Asia, or those in the Arab world. The prophetic word tells us that they all must hear the gospel as it is taught in the Book of Mormon and through the revelations of the restoration. Each will do so in their appointed time and season. The work cannot be rushed. Time and seasoning are required in the making of a true Latter-day Saint. Scripture attests that all are to be accorded the privilege of hearing the gospel declared in their own tongue (see D&C 90:11) and by their own people (see Alma 29:8), and that the time will come when there will be congregations of Saints upon all the face of the earth (see 1 Nephi 14:12). These local congregations will be presided over by those of their own number, whose spiritual stature is that of kings and priests (see

Revelation 5:8–10). Surely Christ will not come until the membership of the Church numbers in the hundreds of millions. Again, the labor has but begun.

The New Jerusalem must be established in Jackson County, Missouri, with a temple of the Lord at its very center. As with the New World, so with the Old: a temple must also be built again in the ancient city of Jerusalem. In the millennial day the law will go forth from the New Jerusalem and the word of the Lord from the Zion of the Old World.

All of these events are to be accomplished in a world filled with turmoil and evil, which will only continue to increase. False prophets and false Christs are to abound, while the hearts of men become increasing indifferent to the things of the Spirit. Wars and rumors of wars will be the constant order of things. As the Church moves into new frontiers, opposition and persecution will be commonplace. The kinds of experience common to both the meridian Church and the early days of this dispensation will repeat themselves. Faith in greater measure than that yet known to the Latter-day Saints will be required. At the same time the veil will become increasingly thin for many, and God will pour out his Spirit upon all flesh; and our sons and daughters will prophesy and see visions, while the old will be favored with dreams divinely sent.

MANY APPEARANCES

The Second Coming will be preceded by a host of comings. Perhaps the best known text is that of Malachi, wherein he promised that the Lord would come suddenly to his temple. We need not suppose that this is a single event or that this prophecy has been fulfilled. Each temple is dedicated to the Lord as his house, and it can only be supposed that he will visit them all. Doctrine and Covenants 133:20 states: "For behold, he shall stand upon the mount of Olivet, and upon the mighty ocean, even the great deep, and upon the islands of the sea, and upon the land of Zion."

"Where, then, will the Lord come, in what places will he stand, and whence shall his voice be heard?" asked Elder Bruce R. McConkie. In response he said,

The Lord, whom we seek, shall suddenly come to his temple, meaning that he will come to the earth, which is his temple, and also that he will come to those holy houses which he has commanded us to build unto his blessed name. Indeed, he came suddenly to the Kirtland Temple on the 3rd day of April in 1836; he has also appeared in others of his holy houses; and he will come in due course to the temples in Jackson County and in Jerusalem. And he will come to his American Zion and his Jewish Jerusalem. His voice will roar forth from both world capitals. He will speak personally, angelic ministrants will proclaim his word, and his mortal servants will speak with his voice. His feet will stand on Olivet on the east of Jerusalem, and he will come with the 144,000 high priests to Mount Zion in America. And where else? Upon the oceans and the islands and the continents, in the land of Zion and elsewhere. The clear meaning is that there will be many appearances, in many places, to many people. And when the day is at hand and the hour has arrived, he will come quickly, as the prophetic word, both ancient and modern, so repetitiously attests. "Surely I come quickly," saith the Lord, to which John replies: "Even so, come, Lord Jesus." (Rev. 22:20).[1]

Among the most notable of the visits of the Lord prior to the Second Coming will be the great meeting to be held at Adam-ondi-Adam, where he will partake of the sacrament with the great prophets of ancient times. Named in revelation are Adam, Joseph, Jacob, Isaac, Abraham, Peter, James, John, and others. "And also with all those whom my Father hath given me out of the world" (D&C 27:14). This statement we would understand to be our invitation to be in attendance if we live the way we have been instructed to live.

HIS COMING WILL BE NO SURPRISE TO THE SAINTS

There certainly is to be no secret relative to the return of Christ, save it be the exact day and hour. His Saints are to be prepared in all things. Scriptural imagery likens his coming to a thief in the night for those who believe not. They are to be caught unaware, but it is not so with those of the household of faith. For them it is to be as the woman about to give birth to a child. That a child is to be born is no surprise to his mother or family; all know the approximate time and wait with anxiousness.

HE WILL COME IN VENGEANCE

As to the actual day of his coming, I but quote the scriptural text:

And it shall be answered upon their heads; for the presence of the Lord shall be as the melting fire that burneth, and as the fire which causeth the waters to boil.

O Lord, thou shalt come down to make thy name known to thine adversaries, and all nations shall tremble at thy presence—

When thou doest terrible things, things they look not for;

Yea, when thou comest down, and the mountains flow down at thy presence, thou shalt meet him who rejoiceth and worketh righteousness, who remembereth thee in thy ways.

For since the beginning of the world have not men heard nor perceived by the ear, neither hath any eye seen, O God, besides thee, how great things thou hast prepared for him that waiteth for thee.

And it shall be said: Who is this that cometh down from God in heaven with dyed garments; yea, from the regions which are not known, clothed in his glorious apparel, traveling in the greatness of his strength?

And he shall say: I am he who spake in righteousness, mighty to save.

And the Lord shall be red in his apparel, and his garments like him that treadeth in the wine-vat.

And so great shall be the glory of his presence that the sun shall hide his face in shame, and the moon shall withhold its light, and the stars shall be hurled from their places.

And his voice shall be heard: I have trodden the wine-press alone, and have brought judgment upon all people; and none were with me;

And I have trampled them in my fury, and I did tread upon them in mine anger, and their blood have I sprinkled upon my garments, and stained all my raiment; for this was the day of vengeance which was in my heart.

And now the year of my redeemed is come; and they shall mention the loving kindness of their Lord, and all that he has bestowed upon them according to his goodness, and according to his loving kindness, forever and ever. (D&C 133:41–52)

At the time of Christ's return we do not want to be found as the unwise virgins with no oil in our lamps. It is for us as a people to be properly prepared to welcome the Savior when he returns, for we have the assurance that he will first come to purge all that is impure from his own house and from among his own people.

[For] vengeance cometh speedily upon the inhabitants of the earth, a day of wrath, a day of burning, a day of desolation, of weeping, of mourning, and of lamentation; and as a whirlwind it shall come upon all the face of the earth, saith the Lord.

And upon my house shall it begin, and from my house shall it go forth, saith the Lord;

First among those among you, saith the Lord, who have professed to know my name and have not known me, and have blasphemed against me in the midst of my house, saith the Lord. (D&C 112:24–26)

CERTAINTY AMID CONFUSION

No event in earth's history is destined to have the transcendent effect on humankind, the earth, and all created things that the Second Coming of Christ will have. At that time all that is wicked, all that is telestial in nature, will be destroyed; and the earth will return to its paradisiacal or Edenic state, in which Christ will rule and reign for a thousand years. Of that time the Lord said,

Every corruptible thing, both of man, or of the beasts of the field, or of the fowls of the heavens, or of the fish of the sea, that dwells upon all the face of the earth, shall be consumed; and also that of element shall melt with fervent heat; and all things shall become new, that my knowledge and glory may dwell upon all the earth. And in that day the enmity of man, and the enmity of beasts, yea, the enmity of all flesh, shall cease from before my face. (D&C 101:24–26)

Could you imagine something of such importance being left to scriptural descriptions that are sufficiently ambiguous that their meaning and intention has been a point of contention for thousands of years among professing Christians? Would you be surprised to learn that the phrase "Second Coming" is nowhere to be found within the covers of the Bible? Generally Bible dictionaries and Bible encyclopedias do not contain entries for this phrase. Discussions of this subject are more often found under the heading "Parousia," the Greek word for "presence" or "advent." *The International Standard Bible Encyclopedia* notes that "the Second Advent of our Lord has been throughout Christian history a perplexity only less than was His First Advent as an anticipation to the Jews," who claimed to be the stewards of the scriptures and totally missed their meaning relative to Christ. Our writer goes on to observe that "no one yet has ever rightly interpreted prophecy *before its fulfillment.*"[2]

It is with a different sense of confidence that we as Latter-day Saints approach this subject, finding much by way of prophecy in the Doctrine and Covenants that amplifies, expands, and expounds on the Old and New Testaments. Uncertainty relative to the return of Christ and his millennial reign are erased by the revelations of the Restoration.[3] Our testimony is sure.

NOTES

1. McConkie, *Millennial Messiah,* 577–78.
2. *International Standard Bible Encyclopedia,* 3:2249.
3. We would particularly note sections 29, 45, 101, and 133.

CHAPTER 25

SEALING YOUR TESTIMONY

WHAT then is your testimony of Christ? It is the composite of all that you know of him by the witness of the Spirit. Your testimony reaches out and embraces all the knowledge that you have of the gospel, for all such principles bear witness of Christ. In the most complete sense, your testimony is your life. It is what you are, what you believe, and what you do not believe; it is what you do and what you choose not to do. Your testimony is a living, breathing thing. You cannot separate belief from action.

This is the reason why it is so hypocritical for someone to say they have studied the history of the Church and found in it too many inconsistencies to believe that the Church is true. The history of the Church is simply an account of things that happened to those who were members of the Church; and if those people died true to the faith, then that is their testimony and that is our history. Do you see it? For those who lived it there were no inconsistencies. Joseph and Hyrum sealed their testimony of the Book of Mormon and the revelations of the Restoration with their blood in the Carthage Jail. You cannot use their history as an excuse to be anything less than faithful. As to what we call history, they lived it; whatever the flaws were, they knew them—they knew them a thousand times better than we ever will—and they died in the faith. They did not waver, they did not doubt, and they did not hedge. When the time came they mounted their horses and rode to Carthage. That was their testimony.

What could be more foolish than reading some fragment of their story as recorded by someone who may or may not have faith and using that as justification to reject that for which these men, so honored of God, both lived and were willing to die?

To Testify of Christ Is to Teach of Christ

What does it mean to bear your testimony? It means to teach or share with others part of the knowledge you have of the gospel of Jesus Christ, doing so under the direction and by the power of the Spirit. It is to make an open attestation or declaration, either orally or in writing, of things you know about Christ and his gospel. In a court of law, an admissible testimony is a declaration of facts relevant to the issue to be decided, given by someone whose knowledge is immediate and personal to the events at issue. Hearsay or secondhand knowledge is not admissible as a testimony. The same standard applies in the realm of spiritual things. Competence as a witness is always predicated on knowledge. Your competence as a witness of Christ embraces all that has been revealed to you to be true as you have studied the scriptures, listened to the gospel taught, taught the gospel and borne your own testimony, and had innumerable other experiences as you have labored in his name.

When we speak of bearing our testimony, we generally have in mind a brief expression of the surety that is ours that

Christ is literally the Son of God, who, through his suffering in Gethsemane and on the cross of Calvary, freed us from all the effects of Adam's fall. Through Christ, we have extended to us the opportunity to obtain eternal life, which we can do on condition of our obedience to the laws and ordinances of his gospel. What we call the bearing of testimony could more aptly be called the sealing of our testimony. A thoughtful reading of scripture reveals what we might call the prophetic pattern in the bearing of testimony, or the placing of a seal on the things we have declared. Let us review the pattern.

TESTIMONY MUST BE BUILT OUT OF TRUTH

In the prophetic pattern, teaching precedes testifying. We must first teach the truth. Having taught the truth, we can then seal what we have taught with the declaration that what we have taught is true. There are no acceptable substitutes for truth. Consider an interesting drama that played itself out in a small Southern courtroom many years ago. The defendant had been indicted and was being tried for murder. The victim had been a man of prominence. The nature of his death was gruesome. The jury had been impaneled and the witnesses duly sworn in. The prosecuting attorney was a man of prominence, eloquence, and distinction. The defense attorney was young and inexperienced. The courtroom was packed. Several days were required to present the evidence, which was placed on a desk before the jury. When the prosecuting attorney stood to make his final summation, a hush filled the courtroom. He explained why he was prosecuting the case, how important maintaining the law was to the survival of society, and the necessity of punishing those guilty of breaking the law. He picked up and displayed each piece of evidence, and as he did so in his wonderful, sonorous voice and with great eloquence, he would assert: "Gentlemen of the jury, these bits of evidence are important. Yes, gentlemen, trifles as light as air are proof as strong as holy writ."

His case was entirely circumstantial, and so it was with particular deliberation that he reviewed each item of evidence to establish a convincing pattern. As he did, he would repeat the refrain with each item, "trifles as light as air are proof as strong as holy writ."

Silence fell over the courtroom as he finished. All present wondered how the young defense attorney would respond. The judge, to relieve the tension, ordered a short recess.

After they reconvened, the judge nodded to the defense attorney and said, "Mr. Attorney, you may proceed."

In a quiet tone he began his argument. He noted how important the role of the jury was in the administering of justice, that only the guilty should be convicted, that circumstantial evidence should be weighed carefully and accepted only when it established the defendant's guilt beyond a reasonable doubt. He spoke to this effect:

"In this case, the testimony is for the most part circumstantial. The items exhibited by the prosecution as he made his address are mere circumstances. The attorney for the prosecution admonished you, more than once, that 'trifles as light as air are proof as strong as holy writ.' That statement is a quotation. You will recall its source. The quotation was not fully or quite accurately stated to you. The quotation, may I remind you, is from Shakespeare's tragedy *Othello*, and may I add that the passage correctly recited should not be 'Trifles as light as air are proof as strong as holy writ,' but 'Trifles light as air are to the jealous confirmations strong as proofs of holy writ.'

"I here pause," he said, "to emphasize the words of that quotation, 'to the jealous'; and to observe that no man on the jury should be or is jealous of my poor defendant. The items—the weapons, the pitiful shoes—which the prosecutor dramatically placed before you, are indeed the merest trifles. They should not have any influence on your verdict.

"Let us recall the scene and the occasion in which these lines were spoken. Iago, as you remember, is playing upon Othello's jealousy, seeking to have him believe that Desdemona, his wife, has been untrue. Iago stands beside Othello, pointing to the planted handkerchief of Desdemona in the possession of Cassio. These are the 'confirmations as strong as holy writ,' said Iago aside. Othello finally, yielding to his jealousy, succumbs to Iago's guile and deceit. Beside himself, he strangles the beautiful, innocent Desdemona. What a wrong."

The young attorney then admonished the jury not to repeat such a wrong. The jury was directed to retire to deliberate. When they returned it was with a verdict of "not guilty," and rightly so.[1]

Something made of nothing is evidence only of nothing. The validity of a testimony is predicated on the substance of which it is made. The testimony which we bear of Christ must consist of principles that are absolute and eternal. They must be true. Falsehoods rendered in the name of Christ are falsehoods still and have no saving power in them. They may be sincerely embraced, wrapped in layers of tradition, and spoken with eloquence in chambers designed to resonate the sound in such a manner as to stir the soul of angels; yet all such trappings cannot make truth of error. Christ, who is the Spirit of truth, can be known only in truth.

The Sanctity of a True Testimony

"The sanctity of a true testimony should inspire a thoughtful care as to its use," stated President Joseph F. Smith.

That testimony is not to be forced upon everybody, nor is it to be proclaimed at large from the housetop. It is not to be voiced merely to "fill up the time" in a public meeting, far less to excuse or disguise the speaker's poverty of thought or ignorance of the truth he is called to expound.

The individual testimony is a personal possession. One cannot give his testimony to another, yet he is able to aid his earnest brother in gaining a true testimony for himself. The over-zealous missionary may be influenced by the misleading thought that the bearing of his testimony to those who have not before heard the gospel message, is to convince or condemn, as the hearers accept or reject. The elder is sent into the field to preach the gospel—the good news of its restoration to earth, showing by scriptural evidence the harmony of the new message with the predictions of earlier times; expounding the truths embodied in the first principles of the gospel; then if he bears his testimony under divine inspiration, such a testimony is as a seal attesting the genuineness of the truths he has declared, and so appealing to the receptive soul whose ears have been saluted by the heaven-sent message.

But the voicing of one's testimony, however eloquently phrased or beautifully expressed, is no fit or acceptable substitute for the needed discourse of instruction and counsel expected in a general gathering of the people. The man who professes a testimony as herein described, and who assumes that his testimony embraces all the knowledge he needs, and who therefore lives in indolence and ignorance shall surely discover his error to his own cost and loss. A gift from God, if neglected, or unworthily used, is in time withdrawn; the testimony of the truth will not remain with one who, having received [it], uses not the sacred gift in the cause of individual and general advancement.[2]

Since a testimony consists of knowledge it can never be used as a substitute for knowledge.

THE HOLY ORDER

The prophetic pattern for teaching and testifying of Christ is given to us by Alma. It can be summarized as follows:

1. We begin by declaring the message of Christ as found in scripture. ("For I am called to speak after this manner, according to the holy order of God, which is in Christ Jesus; yea, I am commanded to stand and testify unto this people the things which have been spoken by our fathers concerning the things which are to come" [Alma 5:44].)

2. We then add to the testimony of the ancients our testimony that we know that what they declared to be true is indeed true, for it has been revealed anew to us in like manner as it was to them. We thus establish the principle that revelation is to be known and understood by the spirit of revelation. ("And this is not all. Do ye not suppose that I know of these things myself? Behold, I testify unto you that I do know that these things whereof I have spoken are

true. And how do ye suppose that I know of their surety? Behold, I say unto you they are made known unto me by the Holy Spirit of God. Behold, I have fasted and prayed many days that I might know these things of myself. And now I do know of myself that they are true; for the Lord God hath made them manifest unto me by his Holy Spirit; and this is the spirit of revelation which is in me. And moreover, I say unto you that it has thus been revealed unto me, that the words which have been spoken by our fathers are true, even so according to the spirit of prophecy which is in me, which is also by the manifestation of the Spirit of God" [Alma 5:45–47].)

3. Having thus familiarized ourselves with the spirit of revelation, we are now able to take the scriptural texts with which we began and expound, enlarge, and apply them by that same Spirit. This means that revelation properly understood will always beget additional revelation. ("I say unto you, that I know of myself that whatsoever I shall say unto you, concerning that which is to come, is true; and I say unto you, that I know that Jesus Christ shall come, yea, the Son, the Only Begotten of the Father, full of grace, and mercy, and truth. And behold, it is he that cometh to take away the sins of the world, yea, the sins of every man who steadfastly believeth on his name" [Alma 5:48].)

These three principles, Alma tells us, constitute the "holy order" after which the gospel is to be taught.

Consider how perfectly these principles are illustrated in this description by Alma of the manner in which the four sons of

Mosiah taught the gospel to the Lamanites. "They [the sons of Mosiah] had waxed strong in the knowledge of the truth; for they were men of a sound understanding and they had searched the scriptures diligently, that they might know the word of God. But this is not all; they had given themselves to much prayer, and fasting; therefore they had the spirit of prophecy, and the spirit of revelation, and when they taught, they taught with power and authority of God" (Alma 17:2–3).

In 1 and 2 Nephi we have fifty-five chapters of instruction relative to the gospel given to us by Nephi. While Nephi knew far more about Christ and his gospel than is therein contained, this is a good representation of his knowledge and understanding of gospel principles. Now, having so taught us, he says, "Hearken unto these words and believe in Christ," which is tantamount to saying, "If you have listened to what I have taught you, then you will know that Jesus is the Christ." He then suggests to his readers that if they do not believe what he has taught about Christ they can simply believe in Christ, for if they believe in Christ they will also believe what Christ has taught. Then—and no one can misunderstand how serious he is about this, since he promises that he and his readers will "stand face to face before his bar," meaning the judgment bar of God—he makes this concluding statement: "For what I seal on earth, shall be brought against you at the judgment bar." That is to say that if you have read these words or had them read to you, you will be accountable for the testimony that Nephi has borne to you (2 Nephi 33:10–11, 15; emphasis added).

Similarly, Moroni, as he concludes the book of Mormon, invites all who read its pages to "come unto Christ, and be perfected in him" and to deny themselves "of all ungodliness; and if ye shall deny yourselves of all ungodliness, and love God with all your might, mind and strength, then is his grace sufficient for you, that by his grace ye may be perfect in Christ; and if by the grace of God ye are perfect in Christ, ye can in nowise deny the power of God." Then, like Nephi, he promises that he will meet all who have heard his word at "the pleasing bar of the great Jehovah, the Eternal Judge of both quick and dead. Amen" (Moroni 10:32, 34). Such is the seal that he places upon that which he has written and compiled. Such is his testimony.

As Latter-Saints we covenanted in the waters of baptism that we would "stand as witnesses of God at all times and in all things, and in all places that [we] may be in" (Mosiah 18:9). As observed above, this does not mean that we are forever forcing our profession of Christ on all who have the fortune—or misfortune, as the case may be—to be in our presence. It does mean, however, that our speech and actions will always be such that the Light of Christ can shine through us. Our actions are our testimony. In all occasions in which we are invited to teach or preach, our testimony is what we teach.

Precious teaching moments ought not to be lost in trivia or simply the teaching of ethical principles. Others can do this. Those possessed with the Holy Ghost ought to do that which requires the Holy Ghost to do. Our divine commission is to teach the doctrines of the restored gospel and to testify of what Christ revealed therein. We ought to speak of those things that are the most attractive to the Holy Ghost, thus assuring his companionship to attest to the truthfulness of what we have said.

"Then after we have taught people the principles of the gospel, after we have let our light shine before them, it remains for us to seal that witness with pure testimony, as moved upon by the Holy Ghost, that we as individuals know that these things are true."[3]

Building Stronger Testimonies

You cannot build a strong testimony out of weak doctrine. History knows of no army that suffered greater deprivation than that experienced by the army that marched under General Washington. They were poorly equipped and often poorly trained; they endured bitter cold and near starvation, along with the death of loved ones, to establish the principle of freedom. Only a people who were used to such hardships could have endured such privation. Our pioneer forefathers were their rightful successors in the exercise of faith under the most trying of circumstances. They were a strong people who had been made strong by constantly doing that which required strength.

No one ever became spiritually strong by doing things that did not require faith, courage, and obedience. All the talk in the world will not negate the necessity of lifting the weights in a strength-training program. As a people we send out thousands of young men to do missionary work. It is hard work, and if we send them out without having first taught them to work hard, we have done them and the missionary cause a great disservice. The principle is absolute and eternal: you cannot develop strength by doing that which is convenient or easy. The pursuit of easy things is the formula for weakness.

Our Knowledge of Christ

The principles that we have reviewed relative to Christ in the preceding chapters constitute strong doctrine. Each principle is unique to the faith of Latter-day Saints. Each principle requires us to stand independent of the world. We have not built the house of our understanding out of the theological rubble from which traditional Christianity has come. Our doctrines are not the result of long debate or the vote of councils,

257

nor do they seek to be validated by popular consent. Our doctrines bear the label "divine revelation." If there had not been a restoration of the gospel we would not have them. They are sweet to the taste; they feel good; and they engender that faith that leads to eternal life.

Every principle that we declare relative to Christ has within itself the evidence of its own truthfulness. Their purity bears witness of their divine origin. They constitute the Latter-day Saint testimony of Christ. They speak of a Christ who is actually and literally the Son of God, a Christ who laid down his body and took it up again in an inseparable union of body and spirit. They speak of a Christ who said to the original Twelve, "Ye have not chosen me, but I have chosen you, and ordained you, that ye should go and bring forth fruit" (John 15:16). All who speak in his name must be commissioned in like manner. They must be called by prophecy and revelation and receive the laying on of hands by those in authority to administer in his name. This is because his house is a house of order. There is but one plan of salvation and one Christ. There is but one "true and living church upon the face of the whole earth" (D&C 1:30).

Our testimony of Christ embraces the verities that he himself testified of his own office and calling and that he requires all men to hear and heed his words. "Therefore it shall come to pass," he said speaking to the Nephites, "that whosoever will not believe in my words, who am Jesus Christ, which the Father shall cause him [Joseph Smith] to bring forth unto the Gentiles, and shall give unto him power that he shall bring them forth unto the Gentiles, (it shall be done even as Moses said) they shall be cut off from among my people who are of the covenant" (3 Nephi 21:11). This is to say that all men must accept his word as it comes from those he has called and commissioned to speak in his stead.

Joseph Smith is the great revelator of Christ for this dispensation. To reject his testimony, his authority, the doctrine that comes through him, is to reject the living Christ. The principle is ever so, "For he that receiveth my servants receiveth me" (D&C 84:36), and those rejecting his servants have rejected him. Such is the seal we place upon our testimony.

Because of the revelations of the Restoration, we have knowledge and understanding about the nature of God and his Son that reach far beyond the comprehension of men. This places us in a greater position of responsibility than others are in, for the testimony we bear of him should reflect these truths and this knowledge. It should also reflect in the way we live. We have no right to be less than the best living people on the face of the earth. There should be a strength and power in the testimony we bear that all the world cannot match.

Elder Jeffrey R. Holland stated the principle thus:

> I've often thought, and I've said to my own children, that those parents who kept going past Chimney Rock and past Martin's Cove (and a few didn't get farther than that) where those little graves are dotted all across the historic landscape of this Church—they didn't do that for a program, they didn't do it for a social activity, they did it because the faith of the gospel of Jesus Christ was in their soul, it was in the marrow of their bones. That's the only way those mothers could bury that baby in a breadbox and move on, saying, "The promised land is out there somewhere. We're going to make it to the valley."
>
> They could say that because of covenants and doctrine and faith and revelation and spirit. If we can keep that in our families and in the Church, maybe a lot of other

things start to take care of themselves. Maybe a lot of other less needed things sort of fall out of the wagon. I'm told those handcarts could only hold so much. Just as our ancestors had to choose what they took, maybe the 21st century will drive us to decide, 'What can I put on this handcart?' It's the substance of our soul; it's the stuff right down in the marrow of our bones. We'll have blessed family and Church if we can cling to the revelations.[4]

It is a sacred privilege to be a Latter-day Saint, to have been baptized by authority for the remission of sins, and under the hands of the priesthood to have been given the gift of the Holy Ghost. Joseph Smith said, "No man can receive the Holy Ghost without receiving revelations."[5] All who possess this gift are expected to be competent witnesses of Christ. It was to this end that we were born and to this end that this gift was given. It is for us, then, above all people on the face of the earth, to know Christ and the saving principles of his gospel and to be prepared to testify of their truthfulness. May the God of heaven bless us that we might be worthy of that trust.

Notes

1. Oberdorfer, "Trifles as Light as Air."
2. Smith, *Gospel Doctrine*, 206.
3. McConkie, Conference Report, Oct. 1948, 27.
4. Holland, Worldwide Leadership Training Meeting, 28.
5. Smith, *Teachings*, 328.

SOURCES

Eiselen, Frederick Carl, Edwin Lewis, and David G. Downey, eds. *The Abingdon Bible Commentary*. Edited by Frederick Carl Eiselen, Edwin Lewis, and David G. Downey. New York: Abingdon Press, 1929.

Ackroyd, P. R., and C. F. Evans, eds. *The Cambridge History of the Bible: From the Beginnings to Jerome*. Vol. 1. Cambridge, United Kingdom: Cambridge University Press, 1980.

Barker, James L. *Apostasy from the Divine Church*. Salt Lake City: Bookcraft, 1960.

Benson, Ezra Taft. *Come Unto Christ*. Salt Lake City: Deseret Book, 1983.

Buck, Charles. *Theological Dictionary*. Philadelphia: J. J. Woodward, 1844.

Clark, J. Reuben Jr. "The Charted Course of the Church in Education." Lecture at Brigham Young University, Aspen Grove, Utah, August 8, 1938.

Cross, F. L. and E. A. Livingstone, eds. *The Oxford Dictionary of the Christian Church*. 2nd ed. rev. Edited by F. L. Cross and E. A. Livingstone. New York: Oxford University Press, 1990.

First Presidency of the Church (Joseph F. Smith, John R. Winder, and Anton H. Lund). "Origin of Man." In *Messages of the First Presidency of the Church of Jesus Christ of Latter-day Saints,* compiled by James R. Clark. 6 vols. Salt Lake City: Bookcraft, 1965–75.

Holland, Jeffrey R. "Roundtable Discussion." *Worldwide Leadership Training Meeting: Building Up a Righteous Posterity,* February 9, 2008.

Hymns of The Church of Jesus Christ of Latter-day Saints. Salt Lake City: The Church of Jesus Christ of Latter-day Saints, 1985.

Journal of Discourses. 26 vols. London: Latter-day Saints' Book Depot, 1854–86.

LDS Bible Dictionary. In *The Holy Bible.* Salt Lake City: The Church of Jesus Christ of Latter-day Saints, 1979.

Leon-Dufour, Xavier. *Dictionary of the New Testament.* San Francisco: HarperSanFrancisco, 1983.

McConkie, Bruce R. Conference Report. October 1948, 48–52.

———. *Doctrinal New Testament Commentary.* 3 vols. Salt Lake City: Bookcraft, 1973.

———. *Millennial Messiah.* Salt Lake City: Deseret Book, 1982.

———. *Mormon Doctrine.* Salt Lake City, Bookcraft, 1966.

———. *A New Witness for the Articles of Faith.* Salt Lake City: Deseret Book, 1985.

———. "Our Relationship with the Lord." Brigham Young University address, March 2, 1982.

———. "The Salvation of Little Children." *Ensign,* April 1977, 3–7.

———. "The Three Pillars of Eternity." Brigham Young University address, February 17, 1981.

Millet, Robert L., and Joseph Fielding McConkie. *The Life Beyond.* Salt Lake City: Deseret Book, 1986.

Oberdorfer, A. Leo. "Trifles as Light as Air." In *The Alabama Lawyer* 15 (July 1954): 290–93.

Orr, James, ed. *The International Standard Bible Encyclopedia.* 5 vols. Grand Rapids, Michigan: Wm. B. Eerdmans, 1988.

Richards, Franklin D., and James A. Little. *A Compendium of the Doctrines of the Gospel.* Rev. ed. Salt Lake City: Deseret Book Co., 1925.

Richards, Larry. *Zondervan Expository Dictionary of Bible Words.* Grand Rapids, Michigan: Zondervan, 1991.

Schonfield, Hugh J., ed. and trans. *The Original New Testament: A Radical Reinterpretation and New Translation.* Edited and translated by Hugh J. Schonfield. New York: HarperCollins, 1985.

Schaff, Philip. *History of the Christian Church.* 8 vols. Grand Rapids: Wm. B. Eerdmans, 1910.

Smith, Joseph. *History of The Church of Jesus Christ of Latter-day Saints.* Edited by B. H. Roberts. 7 vols. Salt Lake City: Deseret Book, 1927.

———. *Lectures on Faith.* Salt Lake City: Deseret Book, 1985.

———. *Teachings of the Prophet Joseph Smith.* Compiled by Joseph Fielding Smith. Salt Lake City: Deseret Book, 1976.

Smith, Joseph F. *Gospel Doctrine.* Salt Lake City: Deseret Book, 1986.

Smith, Joseph Fielding. *Doctrines of Salvation.* Edited by Bruce R. McConkie. 3 vols. Salt Lake City: Bookcraft, 1954.

INDEX

A

Abrahamic covenant, 214–15
Augustine, Saint, 27
accountability, age of, 142
Adam
    as Michael, 20
    testifies of Christ, 51–52
Adam and Eve
    agency of, 38–41
    creation of, 24
    and forbidden fruit, 24
    Latter-day Saint view of, 64, 67
    as myth, 58
    painting of, 30
    transgression of, 42
Adam-ondi-Ahman, 241
agency, 37, 45
    of Adam and Eve, 38–41
Apostles, 157–8
Atonement, 26, 52–53
    as result of Fall, 23, 54–56

B

baptism
    as Christ-oriented ordinance, 73

confusion concerning, 127–28
    modern revelations concerning,
        74–75
    of Jesus, 75–76
    symbolism of, 23, 73–74
    See also infant baptism, baptism
        for the dead
baptism for the dead, 100
Bible, traditional Christian view of
    130–31, 197
Book of Mormon
    as "new covenant," 135
    as witness of Christ, 92, 125
    key to gathering of Israel, 202

C

Calvinism, 31–35
children
    innocence of, 138
    Jesus ministers to, 138–39
    salvation of, 140–41
Christianity, definition of, 91
circumcision, 72–73
Council of Trent. *See* Trent,
    Council of